Contents

Published by Evans Brothers Limited
2A Portman Mansions
Chiltern Street
London W1M 1LE

Copyright © 1990 Casterman, originally published in French under the title Les Jours de l'Histoire: La Guerre de Cent Ans

English translation copyright
© Evans Brothers Limited 1993

English translation by arrangement with Bookdeals Translations
PO Box 263
Taunton TA3 6RH
UK

Maps by Michael Welply

Published by agreement with Casterman, Belgium

Printed in Hong Kong

ISBN 0 237 51278 5

EVANS HISTORY LIBRARY

THE AGE OF REASON

Sylvie Chaperon

English translation by Anton Wills-Eve

Illustrations by Jean-Michel Payet

Œconomie Rustique,
Mouches à Miel.

Evans Brothers Limited

Foreword

The Age of Reason is the name given to the period 1715 to 1789 which saw the development of many new ideas, inventions and discoveries which changed the face of European society. These changes gave ordinary people the wealth and freedom to try out political and social reforms which, for the first time, dealt with what we think of today as basic human rights. However, many of these reforms faced fierce opposition from absolute monarchies and the Church.

During this period, people used their powers of reasoning to make great steps forward in many fields. In the world of science people began to work out the laws which governed the natural world and the universe. By observation, exploration and experimentation great advances were made in medicine, geographical discovery and appreciation of the true size and make-up of the world. Knowledge of physics, chemistry and botany almost doubled between 1700 and 1800. And the agricultural and industrial revolutions, which made it possible to feed, clothe, house and transport ever larger populations, pushed forward the technological advancement which is still going on today.

The political and economic changes which occurred in every Western country throughout the century were also vitally important. Before 1700 the terrible wars of religion, which had ravaged Europe since the Protestant Reformation and the Roman Catholic Counter Reformation in the middle of the sixteenth century, had made it virtually impossible for peace to last for long anywhere. Only Britain, which underwent civil war from 1642 to 1660 followed by parliamentary rule under a constitutional monarchy, and The Netherlands had anything close to a liberal or free-thinking society by 1715.

So by 1715, when George I had ascended the British throne as the first king of the House of Hanover, three main challenges faced Europe: how to narrow the huge divide between rich and poor, how to create economic prosperity and how to establish a fully liberal society in which new ideas could flourish without having to pass the censorship of Church and monarchy.

Ignorance, or lack of education, existed in varying degrees throughout the continent. The movement which set out to rectify this in France is known as the Enlightenment, and the ideas of the French writers, who tried to develop political, economic and social equality, spread all over Europe.

Yet by 1789, Britain was the most powerful nation in the Western world. For, although Europe was still a lively centre of culture and ideas, all the hopes for social equality had only resulted in more nationalistic governments in Austria, Russia and Prussia. In spite of the number of colonies they possessed, the influence of Spain and The Netherlands had waned, while a republic had been set up in the United States of America. And France was about to experience a bloody and horrific revolution.

The Sun King's Legacy

After a long illness Louis XIV of France, the "Sun King", died on September 1, 1715, and France began a period of very unusual mourning. Seldom can a country have been more elated to hear of its king's death. Although the courtiers and nobility filed past the coffin with solemn respect, few of them hid their relief at the end of an era in which fashionable life at Versailles had been ruled with superficial pomp and ceremony. In some places people let their feelings show, holding spontaneous celebrations in villages and towns and even firework displays and fêtes! Most of Europe was equally glad to see the old king die, for France had extended its national boundaries during Louis' reign. Louis had had to make overseas concessions to England, in Canada and some of the territories of North America: notably Acadia (modern Nova Scotia), Newfoundland and Hudson Bay. However, at home he had gained possession of Dunkirk, some of Flanders, Strasbourg and the Franche-Compté.

Unfortunately, as Louis himself admitted, this king was too fond of making war. And, more importantly, his great and long-standing ambition to strengthen the power of France had caused several European powers to form alliances against him. His subjects had had to bear all the expense and hardships of the seemingly endless wars. Their income had been greatly reduced by ever-increasing taxes and they had been worn down by food shortages and frequent epidemics. The Treaty of Utrecht (1713) attempted to end these European wars once and for all, with the balance of power being shared by Britain, France and Austria.

Three countries most benefited from the struggles up to 1713. Britain took

over almost all the Dutch sea routes and overseas possessions worth having. Prussia quietly began to build up a kingdom and an army. The third, Russia, gradually gained land and power at the expense of both Poland, whose elective system of monarchy made government almost impossible, and Sweden, which saw large tracts of Baltic possessions disappear after the death of its soldier-king, Charles XII.

The long years of absolute monarchy had considerably strengthened the centralised power of the Crown in France, to the envy of many European monarchs. However the nobility were interested only in their own pleasure, and they controlled both the parliaments (the regional law courts) and all senior administrative posts throughout the kingdom, and even the pope had given way to Louis over the appointment of senior clergy and the running of the Roman Catholic Church in France. Peasant uprisings early in

the reign had been stamped out and by 1715 a strict moral tone had been imposed on all aspects of national and public life.

Yet cultural life was starting to break out of these strict confines and a new freedom of thought was emerging. Several fringe writers questioned religious orthodoxy, while a thirst for knowledge and a hunger for rational explanation permeated all aspects of academic life. All sorts of subjects and ideas were discussed and explored. People travelled to countries as far afield as Persia, China and Lapland and began to write about the "primitive peoples" of the world. Benedict de Spinoza's great work, *Ethics*, was published a few weeks after his death, in 1677. It showed religion and despotism as two conniving authorities which controlled people ready to believe in them for their own ends. Thus began, very slowly at first, the European crisis of conscience.

The end of a reign. In this painting a portrait of Louis XIV is being stored away in the gallery of Gersaint, one of the leading Parisian art dealers. The philosophers of the Age of Reason rejected the late king's ideas on absolutism. But as the eighteenth century advanced they acknowledged that Louis had been a patron of the arts. Even Voltaire devoted a monumental work to him entitled The Century of Louis XIV. (Detail from Gersaint's Gallery, *by Watteau, Louvre Museum, Paris.)*

Economic Problems in Britain and France

One overriding problem faced both Britain and France at this time. Each country had an enormous national debt as a result of the recent wars. In Britain it stood at 51 million pounds and in France at three and a half billion livres (about £140 million). Both countries tried to solve their problems the same way.

In Britain the South Sea Company, which had been given greatly increased trading privileges by the Treaty of Utrecht, offered to buy up the national debt. The company reasoned that, as its profits would soar under the new trading conditions, it could easily sell its shares, and offered the government £7,500,000 towards paying off any creditors who did not want to exchange their loans for shares in the company.

As financiers could only demand the interest on their huge loans to the national debt, the scheme proved very attractive – many people made their fortunes as the value of £100 shares rose on the stock market until they were worth more than £1,000. The buying and selling of shares in the South Sea Company became a craze, but the bubble eventually burst. This was not because the company failed to make a profit on its trading, but because many fraudulent companies were set up claiming to sell South Sea shares, when they were worthless. As investors realised this they tried to cash in their shares immediately, and in 1720 the entire company went bankrupt, bringing the downfall of the government. This crisis brought Robert Walpole to power. As the leading minister he became known as the prime minister (from the French word for first, "premier"), now the usual title for

Robert Walpole (1676-1745). (Mary Evans Picture Library.)

Britain's head of government.

In France, the Duke of Orléans, who ran the affairs of Crown and state, turned for advice to his Scottish friend and financial adviser John Law. Law developed a scheme which came to be known as "The System". In 1716 he set up his own bank which issued its own notes that could be used to pay taxes. He then founded companies which sold shares to pay for expeditions to French colonies to search for gold, silver and mineral deposits. He promised untold wealth from gold and diamond mines in the Mississippi basin.

As in Britain, people were caught up in the fever of share speculation, hoping to make their fortunes overnight. But when a rumour spread through Paris that there was no gold in the Mississippi, the System's days were numbered. Within a few weeks all the shareholders tried to cash in their shares, which the bank could not redeem. The System went bankrupt and Law fled the country.

These experiences made many people in Britain and France wary of share dealings. But some good did come out of the affairs. The national debts of both countries were greatly reduced and increased investment in overseas colonies created a boom in the maritime industry with the emergence of trading companies. Colonising other countries was expensive, but great profits could be made by bringing back products like coffee and tea to sell in Europe.

Interest in overseas exploration led to the publication of such books as *Robinson Crusoe*, by Daniel Defoe (1719). The subject lent itself to political satire, of which Jonathan Swift's *Gulliver's Travels* (1726) was the best example. With economic recovery in Britain and France the Regency period became one of greater freedom in both conduct and thought.

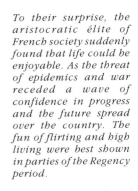

To their surprise, the aristocratic élite of French society suddenly found that life could be enjoyable. As the threat of epidemics and war receded a wave of confidence in progress and the future spread over the country. The fun of flirting and high living were best shown in parties of the Regency period.

The Agricultural Revolution

Sown in rotation with cereals, root crops took hardly any goodness out of the soil. They also provided nourishing fodder for cattle.

The farming expert and Secretary to the Board of Agriculture, Arthur Young, travelled all over England studying agricultural methods. He wrote detailed accounts of his journeys, and it is from these reports that we get much of our picture of the state of rural life and the improvements in farming methods which were developed in the eighteenth century.

The most important change in agricultural methods at this time was the move away from open to enclosed fields. A growing population required more and more food and more efficient ways of growing that food were sought. In 1700 about 60 per cent of farmland in Britain was arranged in the open field system. Under this system a farmer's land was made up of lots of strips of ground scattered over a large area. He would also have had access to the common land, a large area of waste land which all local people had the right to use. With enclosure, all of the farm land, including the common land, was rearranged and divided up into separate fields.

Enclosure Acts began in about 1740 to solve disputes in areas in which not all landowners wanted enclosure. If those who wanted enclosure owned at least 80 per cent of the land, they could get permission from parliament to force enclosure on their neighbours. Because wealthier landowners owned by far the lion's share of the land, these Acts most benefited them. The legal and practical expenses of enclosing land ruined many of the small landowners who had to sell their allotments and work as labourers for a landlord. The loss of the common land, where people could collect berries and firewood or graze cattle or sheep for free, was also a blow to all of the poorer rural communities. Although Arthur Young was very much in favour of enclosures he saw from his travels that, as he said, "By 19 out of every 20

enclosure acts the poor were greatly injured".

However, enclosures brought more positive than negative changes. Enclosures made possible the use of improved methods of farming. The system of crop rotation improved yields and increased the area of land being cultivated at any one time. The quality of products improved and the general economy, as well as the tenant farmers, benefited from the increase in profits which followed this increase in output. Improved technology and methods allowed a small proportion of the workforce to provide greater amounts of food for the growing population. Agriculturalists such as Jethro Tull, who invented the seed drill, and Robert Bakewell, who improved the breeding of livestock such as cattle and sheep, helped to change farming in Britain dramatically.

The old rural community was completely changed. Moderately well-off farm workers might be able to rent

or even own newly-enclosed farms of their own. But the poorer peasants either had to work as labourers for a landlord, or else give up farming altogether and seek work in the rapidly expanding industrial towns.

The introduction of better grazing crops led to the enclosing of pasture for specialist animal farming. New ways of selective breeding meant that farmers could choose animals specifically for the best features, like the quality of their wool or meat.

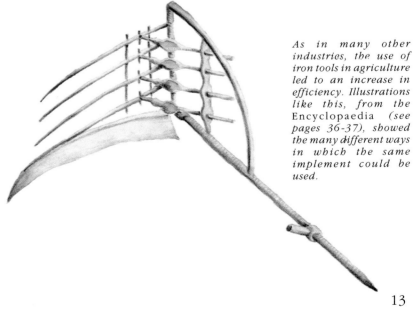

As in many other industries, the use of iron tools in agriculture led to an increase in efficiency. Illustrations like this, from the Encyclopaedia (see pages 36-37), showed the many different ways in which the same implement could be used.

The Population Boom

In the eighteenth century childbirth was very much women's business. Men were pushed into the background as all the female relatives of a mother-to-be arrived to help out at the birth. However, the medical profession was beginning to get involved. Until this time women, left to themselves, had relied upon a mixture of common sense, superstitions and advice handed down from mother to daughter. Now the most competent women from the villages, recommended by the priest or squire, were being sent to follow courses in childbirth. They became the first professional midwives and the number of mothers surviving childbirth increased. This important step forward in practical obstetrics played only a small part in what became this century's population boom. After a long period of stagnation the population of northern and western Europe started to show a steady growth.

The population of England rose from six million in 1700 to nine million in 1800. In France the proportion of the increase was the same, rising from 19 million to 27 million. The population of Europe doubled from 90 million to 180 million during the century. However, the birth rate was about the same in the eighteenth century as it had been in the seventeenth. Most women still had an average of five or six children. The most important cause of the population increase was that more and more babies were surviving infancy. Although the infant mortality rate was still high, it was decreasing all the time. People lived longer because there were better living

conditions and more food. With the improved harvests, famine almost died out. If the wheat crop failed, the potato crop or corn harvest could now replace it. Equally importantly, epidemics such as plague, which had been rife for the past 400 years, started to disappear. And with great advances in medical science during the eighteenth century many epidemic illnesses disappeared altogether. The use of quinine as a medicine became widespread, surgical techniques were improved and the first preventive medicines were being developed. In 1796, Edward Jenner successfully vaccinated a child against smallpox. These advances put as much as ten years on the average life expectancy.

The pressure an increased population put upon both urban and rural communities was both the cause and the result of the technological advances in industry and agriculture of the time as well as advances in the world of medicine.

Weddings were very important events which brought together all the generations of the family and included the whole household: parents, brothers, sisters and servants. In the countryside marriages were often arranged between families. In the towns sons and daughters were more likely to be allowed to choose their own bride or groom. (The Village Betrothal, by Greuze. Louvre Museum, Paris.)

In most families the birth of a son was considered a greater blessing than a daughter. Only a son could carry on the family name. This was particularly important in royal families to secure succession to the throne. During the eighteenth century fashions in baby clothes began to change. For the first time boys were put into trousers instead of dresses, to differentiate them from girls. (An eighteenth century engraving, depicting the joy with which families greeted the birth of a boy.)

15

The British Example

Britain, with its constitutional monarchy and comparative religious tolerance, set the example for a new and enlightened Europe at this time. The smooth running of parliament was by no means as simple as many admirers thought, but in a Europe which was largely absolutist, the British Isles seemed to stand out as the great exception.

By the late seventeenth century, following civil war and revolutions, the power of the monarchy had been greatly diminished. The king could no longer make laws, he could merely approve or reject them. Nor could he levy taxes or muster an army without parliamentary approval. Thus every important decision of government needed parliamentary support.

Elections to the House of Commons were not always fair, especially in the smaller boroughs where an influential local family could often nominate and secure the election of their candidate. In some places candidates would hire groups of voters to ensure success in the elections.

Parliament was made up of two "houses". The House of Lords was composed of peers of the realm and bishops. The Crown appointed bishops and could also create peers. Titles, except in the case of bishops, were hereditary. Despite its great prestige, the Lords played a minor role in government. It could not introduce bills but only debate and vote on legislation proposed by the Commons. The House of Lords was the highest court of justice and appeal in the land.

In the countryside only men over 21 of considerable wealth were allowed to vote for members of the House of Commons. The result of this ruling was that most "county seats" were controlled by big landowners. In towns and boroughs there was not one single qualification for voting. The confusion in voting systems left these elections open to corruption. English constituencies consisted of county seats, for which each of the 40 counties could choose two members, and 204 cities and boroughs were represented by 409 members. Another 69 members represented Scotland, Ireland and Wales. Most constituency boundaries had not been changed since the Middle Ages and this led to abuses such as the "rotten boroughs". These were towns with few inhabitants that had the right to send two members to Westminster. One was Old Sarum in Wiltshire, owned by the Pitt family, which had only one voter who could choose two members of parliament.

Members were elected for a term of seven years and, once installed in Westminster, they gradually started to form two separate parties – though not in the sense of party politics today. These were the "Whigs" (a derogatory term for Scottish bandits), who largely supported parliamentary supremacy in everything, and the "Tories" (a slang term for Irish brigands), who supported the rights of the monarchy and the Church of England. The House of Commons voted bills into law, ratified treaties, levied taxes and controlled the army.

In spite of its shortcomings, this system did succeed in dividing power effectively between the monarchy and parliament. But in practice the famous saying "there is not a blade of grass in the kingdom which is not represented at Westminster" was not quite true and many reforms were still to come. One reform already established was *Habeas Corpus*, which gave everyone the right to a fair trial, allowed freedom of the press and freedom of movement, the right to hold meetings and public gatherings and the right to petition the king or parliament.

During the eighteenth century the move towards a genuine parliamentary democracy was greatly strengthened by the arrival of the Hanoverian dynasty. When Queen Anne, the last Stuart monarch, died the throne was offered to the German Elector of Hanover, who became George I (1714–1727). As he spoke no English at all, and his son George II (1727–1760) was by no means fluent in it at first, the role of the prime minister became more and more important in British politics. Consequently the great prime ministers of the period, like Robert Walpole and William Pitt the elder, relied on support in parliament in order to govern.

Two people held key positions in the House of Commons. The Speaker presided over debates and had the casting vote in the case of deadlock. The Leader of the House was the chief representative of the government and it was his task to defend its actions and policies.

The European Power Struggle (1733-1763)

Maria Theresa (1717-1780) was the Empress of Austria and wife of the Holy Roman Emperor, Francis I. Her struggle to keep her Hapsburg family lands and titles played a key part in all the continental wars from 1730 until her death. (e t Archive.)

In the eighteenth century most of the royal families of Europe were related to each other through marriage which created many problems in terms of succession. Whenever a king, prince or an emperor died there were nearly always two or three rival claimants to his title. This was the legacy of the policy of the Bourbon and Hapsburg families – the main royal dynasties in Europe for the past 150 years – who had carved up the continent between them. So in 1733, when King Augustus II of Poland died, the War of the Polish Succession saw Spain and France supporting one candidate and the Austrian Holy Roman Emperor, Charles VI, supporting another. This war dragged on until 1738.

Charles VI was the last male of the Austrian branch of the House of Hapsburg. He wanted to ensure that his daughter, Maria Theresa, would keep all his possessions after his death, even though by law a woman could not become emperor. So he drew up a document called the "Pragmatic Sanction", and persuaded most other European countries to agree to it. Under its terms Maria Theresa's husband, Francis Stephen, would become Emperor but she would inherit the Hapsburg lands. However, after Charles VI died in 1740, two main events led to what became known as the War of the Austrian Succession. Firstly, the electors of the Holy Roman Empire chose Charles Albert, Elector of Bavaria, to be emperor, taking the title Charles VII. Secondly, most other European leaders decided to ignore the Pragmatic Sanction and tried to conquer as much Hapsburg territory as they could.

The Holy Roman Empire, now effectively the Austrian Empire, consisted primarily of Austria, Bohemia, Silesia, Tyrol, Hungary, Milan and the Austrian Netherlands. The main threats came from Prussia, Bavaria, Saxony, France and Spain. Philip V of Spain wanted to recapture Milan, which his family had lost at the start of the century. Frederick II of Prussia had his eye on Silesia, the key border provinces between his kingdom and Austria. Louis XV of France wanted the Austrian Netherlands (modern Belgium). The electors of Saxony and

Bavaria had strong hereditary claims to the Austrian Empire, as their wives were nieces of Charles VI. In 1743 Britain and The Netherlands eventually joined in on the Austrian side, to protect their own interests.

In 1745 Charles VII died and Francis Stephen finally became emperor, at last making Maria Theresa Empress of Austria. Yet the war dragged on until the Treaty of Aix-la-Chapelle was signed in 1748. As a result of this, Prussia kept Silesia and Spain gained Parma and Piacenza, in Italy, but otherwise Maria Theresa retained most of her inheritance.

The peace of 1748 was little more than a truce, as Maria Theresa was determined to recapture Silesia. Hostilities broke out again in 1756, when the Seven Years' War began. Austria needed a strong ally against the Prussians and, although France had been its enemy for over 300 years, lengthy negotiations led to them becoming allies. As Britain and France were still fighting each other overseas, Britain supported Prussia. Russia took advantage of the confusion to extend its empire westwards, especially in Poland.

The Seven Years' War ended with two separate treaties in 1763. The Treaty of Hubertsburg, between Prussia, Russia and Austria, allowed the Prussians possession of Silesia, but left Russia a much stronger power in Europe than at any time in its history. The Treaty of Paris mainly settled colonial disputes.

But even after 1763 the question of supremacy in central Europe remained unresolved. Prussia and Austria continued to oppose each other. They took turns to ally themselves with Russia and so obtained parts of Poland, which was partitioned three times. Eventually this led to the birth of modern Germany and Russia and completely changed the balance of power in Europe.

All branches of the Bourbon families in Europe loved hunting. The aristocracy set great store by their performances in this pastime in which good horsemanship and shooting skills assured social success. In times of peace hunting took the place of fighting.

19

Free Trade

In France controls by the interior ministry severely hampered trade. Tolls had to be paid on canals and roads. Merchants in towns or fairs could even tax merchandise again when selling it.

Adam Smith (1723-1790) was a Scottish economist. (Medallion by Tassie, The National Portrait Gallery of Scotland.)

The great increase in trade, progress in industry and modernisation of agricultural methods in the eighteenth century laid the foundations for our modern economic system. Philosophers and governments became more and more preoccupied with studying economic theories. A variety of new ideas for increasing national wealth were constantly being debated.

At the start of the century the theory of mercantilism was universally accepted. It was believed that a nation's wealth lay solely in the amount of money that it possessed, and this was measured by the amount of gold and silver it owned. This, in turn, was determined by its balance of trade. Limiting imports, which took money out of the country, and encouraging exports, which brought in foreign capital, was considered the only way to increase reserves of gold and silver.

In the Age of Reason mercantilist policies were common throughout Europe. For example, Charles III of Spain and the Russian czars protected their own trading positions by imposing high tariffs and forming exclusive trading companies. The strict trading conditions imposed on colonies and overseas territories benefited colonial powers. Colonies were forced to sell their goods at low prices to their parent country and also to buy all their imports from it.

Europe's gold and silver reserves came mainly from Brazil and Mexico, as the world production in precious metals soared. But, as world trade increased, the reserves of precious metals were insufficient to finance all the transactions. This was when banks, whether state institutions, as in England and The Netherlands, or private companies, started to play a key role. In exchange for deposits of gold, silver or coinage they issued bankers' drafts. Depositors could cash these in full or part when they needed money. The banks knew from experience that all the people holding such notes were never likely to present them at the same time. This allowed banks to issue notes to a greater total value than their gold and silver reserves. This meant that the value of notes in circulation was far greater than that of the coinage available.

Bank notes gradually became the normal way to settle bills. In a business deal between British and overseas traders the only financial transaction needed was the payment of bills at the end of the deal. This greatly simplified the financing of business and the international transfer of funds.

As trading and manufacturing companies grew, stock markets began to appear. By using these, people could purchase shares in business enterprises in exchange for an annual dividend or share of the profits. The selling of shares provided the money to run and develop a business. The profits and share values of businesses were quoted on the stock exchange. Thus, according to the success of the company, shares would rise or fall in value. Many people, especially bankers and stockbrokers, started making a living simply by buying and selling shares. Naturally, these speculators made fortunes or suffered losses depending on their ability to forecast share values.

The stock exchanges and banks in London and Amsterdam were the best known and most credit-worthy. France lagged a long way behind, due largely to the fact that the Roman Catholic Church was opposed to all forms of usury, or the charging of unnecessarily high interest on loans. Only foreigners to France, like the Scotsman John Law (see page 11), or the Swiss Jacques Necker, tried to introduce modern economic practices there.

The father of modern economics was the Scottish economist Adam Smith (1723-1790). In his essay *The Wealth of Nations*, he put forward the theory that economics operated, like the laws of nature, on the principle of supply and demand. He believed that any economy prospered best without controls or outside interference. The manufacturer wanted the best price for his product, the merchant or middle-man wanted to make as much money as he could and the consumer wanted the best goods at the cheapest price. Smith argued that if these three parts of the business equation were allowed to sort out their own interests they would end up with the best possible deal for all. This was why he advocated a policy of government non-intervention in the process of supply and demand. However, it was a long time before protectionist economic policies were modified enough for his ideas to be put into practice.

In the eighteenth century Britain finally established itself as a leading maritime power. The thriving trade in the port of London made the capital, whose population numbered over one million, one of Europe's leading ports.

The Start of the Industrial Revolution

At the beginning of the eighteenth century people began to develop new ways of making and using metals. All the inventions of the time needed metal parts and so a great deal had to be produced. Soon the use of steam power made it necessary for industries to be near water and coalfields. The next century saw the spread of what is known as the "Black Country". This was the part of England where both water and coal were available, so industry could thrive.

The Industrial Revolution began in Britain in the eighteenth century. The improvements in agriculture and the creation of overseas colonies provided a guaranteed and abundant supply of cheap raw materials like wool, hemp and cotton. Because the country was wealthy there was both an increased demand for all sorts of goods and the capital needed to invest in manufacturing them. Also, as a result of the Enclosures Acts, many agricultural labourers were out of work and had flocked to the towns in search of employment. Manufacturers saw the opportunity to sell these goods to the increasing population at home or to the new overseas colonies at a large profit. It was a combination of all of these things that sparked off the industrial revolution.

Before this time, most manufacturing industries were centred around the home. Agricultural workers ran cottage industries using their own families. They bought their own materials, made their own tools and sold their products at the local market. All sorts of goods, like shoes and knives, were made in this way. However, as the population increased so did the demand for such goods and the cottage industries could not produce enough. Merchants, drapers and ironmongers began to set up businesses in poorer areas, where they bought up quantities of the locally-manufactured goods at very low prices. Eventually these merchants took over from the family cottage industries. They bought raw materials, employed workers, built and ran the first factories, hired out more sophisticated tools to people working from home and sold the finished products.

Sometimes, to speed up production, a businessman would get all his workers together in one building so that he could divide up the work between them more efficiently. Such places were called manufactures and they later became known as mills or factories. Yet even in this way they could not keep up with the growing demand for goods. It was only by using the new machines, which made it possible for all sorts of materials to be produced faster and more cheaply, that demand could be met.

Before the introduction of new machinery in the textile industry, a piece of cloth could be made no wider than the span of a man's arms. John Kay's flying shuttle, which he invented in 1733, enabled the frame on which cotton was spun to be much broader. Because the flying shuttle wove the yarn very quickly it became necessary to find faster ways of spinning. In 1764 James Hargreaves invented the Spinning Jenny. It was improved by Sir Richard Arkwright in 1769, and Samuel Crompton's Spinning Mule was developed from it in 1779. These last two machines were too big to be used in cottages, and this led, in 1781, to Arkwright building the first modern factory to house his machines.

The iron and steel industry also underwent enormous changes at this time. In 1709 Abraham Darby used coke, which was derived from coal, for the first time in his ironworks at Coalbrookdale. By 1779 the first iron bridge in the world had been built there. Coke was used in large amounts in metal casting and could be used for iron or steel. This increased the demand for coal which caused problems in the mining industry. As the mines were dug deeper, water gathered in them which had to be pumped away into underground shafts. This problem was solved in 1712 by Thomas Newcomen's invention, a steam pump to drain mines. It was the first cylinder and piston driven engine ever used. Then, in 1765, James Watt, working at Glasgow University, invented the steam condenser, which greatly improved the performance of the steam engine and reduced the amount of energy needed to run it. He went on to develop a steam engine with a rotary action which could be used to power other machines.

In 1775 a Birmingham ironmaster, Matthew Boulton, talked Watt into working with him. Boulton used his works to produce the machines that Watt was developing. The Boulton and Watt company came up with a very shrewd business idea. They offered to replace, free of charge, the old Newcomen engines with Watt's new machines. In return they asked for one third of the money saved by the mine owners once they had started using the new invention. This proved to be very profitable. From the Chacewater mine alone, which used just three machines, they received more than 60,000 pounds a year!

Soon the steam engine was being used in all kinds of factories, powering everything from looms to mills and steam-hammers to paddle boats. It was this great advance which made Britain the leading industrial power in the world, and kept it well ahead of all its rivals for a long time.

The textile industry was totally changed by the invention of many new machines. During the eighteenth century riots often broke out among skilled workers because they were being replaced by the machines.

Life in the Towns

The dramatic increase in the birth rate saw the populations of many European countries double. But the greatest rise in population – sometimes up to 400 per cent – was in the cities and towns, and the capital cities showed the biggest increases of all. London's population passed the million mark and Paris had some 700,000 inhabitants by the end of the eighteenth century.

The urban population, which only accounted for some 20 per cent of the total population of north-west Europe, was made up of a great variety of people, in terms of both class and income. The aristocracy were still the most important citizens and had town houses and palaces, to which they moved for part of the year to escape the boredom of their stately homes or castles in the countryside. In the great trading ports or industrial centres such as London, Bristol, Manchester and Liverpool, the middle-classes also had their own hierarchy. Merchants, bankers, shop-keepers, shipping agents and farmers mixed with the nobility, members of parliament and holders of high state office.

Whatever the source of their wealth anyone who could afford to would imitate the aristocracy by building sumptuous houses. This in turn created work for architects, builders and interior decorators. Beautiful flooring, mirrors, glasswork, carved doorways and wooden panelling abounded in these new dwellings, which also housed armies of servants. This wealthy sector of society set the fashion in everything from clothes to the theatre and the arts. In the evening their

carriages would roll over the cobbles taking them to an opera, a play, a concert or a ball.

But in many of the houses in the large cities, people from all levels of society could be found. On the first two floors were the apartments of the top professional classes like lawyers, accountants, doctors or wealthy merchants. They usually owned their apartments which they furnished with taste, but not too expensively. Many would have only two or three servants and sometimes just one housekeeper would do all the work. Above them lived the lower middle-classes and craftsmen: tailors, cobblers, bakers and cabinet makers. As often as not they would rent the shop on the ground floor and two or three rooms in the building, where the master-craftsman lived with his family and his apprentices. The attics and garrets housed the poorer workers: washer-women, roofers, handymen, servants and street traders. They had to make do with just one room for their whole family and with a minimum of furniture.

Then the city itself was divided into rich and poor areas. In London the

aristocracy lived mainly on the western side, the area known as Mayfair today. The wealthier merchants and lawyers lived in new developments to the north, modern Marylebone and Bloomsbury, while the poorest classes inhabited the East End and dock areas.

However, as the reforming spirit grew, efforts were made to improve town living conditions. New roads were made wider and lighter. They were given names and houses were given numbers. Concern for human hygiene gradually brought changes. Graveyards were moved to uninhabited areas, and anti-social workplaces, such as abattoirs and tanneries, were situated on the outskirts of the cities.

Old Horse Guards Parade. This famous painting by Antonio Canaletto (1697-1768) captures the colourful and relaxed life enjoyed by upper class society in mid-eighteenth century London. (The Bridgeman Art Library.)

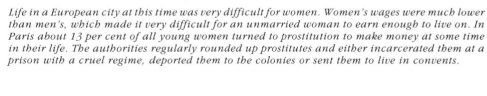

Life in a European city at this time was very difficult for women. Women's wages were much lower than men's, which made it very difficult for an unmarried woman to earn enough to live on. In Paris about 13 per cent of all young women turned to prostitution to make money at some time in their life. The authorities regularly rounded up prostitutes and either incarcerated them at a prison with a cruel regime, deported them to the colonies or sent them to live in convents.

25

Anglo-French Rivalry

Ever since the time of Marlborough, who had regularly thwarted French ambitions by his military victories in Europe at the very start of the eighteenth century, Britain and France had been engaged in a long struggle for supremacy in world trade and colonial influence.

Britain had a growing empire of colonies in the Americas and India. In 1743, Britain joined The Netherlands to help Austria in the war in Europe to make sure that the French armed forces were stretched to their limit on the continent and could not afford to fight overseas colonial campaigns as well. However, at the end of the War of the Austrian Succession Britain and France came to a far from satisfactory agreement, merely returning the conquests they had made in each other's colonies.

By 1756 Britain's colonial ambitions were closer to fulfilment. In the Seven Years' War two different sides were formed from those that had fought the Austrian War of Succession: Britain joined Prussia and Hanover against Austria, France, Russia and, after 1761, Spain. Britain wanted to gain as much control of all overseas territories as possible.

The British suffered an early defeat when the French captured Minorca, in the Mediterranean. But, as the war progressed, the British navy gained a strategically important victory over the French. The battle of Quiberon Bay, off the coast of Brittany, in 1759 resulted in a naval blockade of all French routes to the Atlantic. This meant that France could not reinforce or supply its troops in India, Canada and America, and the British soon captured all of these areas. Canada fell in 1760, soon after General Wolfe had captured Quebec the previous autumn. The last French fortress in India was taken by the English, under Robert Clive, in 1761. Britain's naval supremacy meant that it could keep

French trading vessels off the high seas, or at least out of some of the more lucrative trading ports, which in time severely strained the French economy.

The Treaty of Paris in 1763, between Britain, Spain and France, sealed the British military and diplomatic triumphs overseas. France gave Britain all its possessions in North America, east of the Mississippi, with the exception of New Orleans and some islands in the West Indies, but it kept some of its fishing rights on the St Lawrence river in Canada. France also renounced its Indian territories, although it was allowed to keep trading stations at Pondicherri, Mahé and Chandernagar, providing they were kept unfortified. Minorca was returned to Britain in exchange for the island of Belle Isle, captured by the British in 1761.

These wars resulted in Britain becoming the strongest European naval power in the Far East and North America, and indeed the main colonial power in the world. The East India Company, which regulated British affairs in India for the government, was the envy of every colonial power in the West. Britain's trading empire flourished, virtually unchallenged, until the wars of American Independence, when the United States won the right to self-government.

During the eighteenth century the British kept their prisoners of war in bulks. These were old, unseaworthy ships anchored off the coast or in river estuaries.

Captain Cook

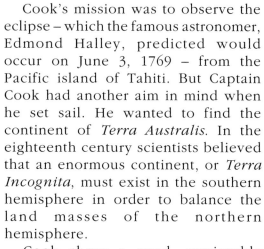

August 26, 1768 was a great day in the life of James Cook. At the age of 40, this relatively unknown English naval officer, son of a Yorkshire farm worker, gave the order for his ship to set sail from Plymouth for the Pacific. On board *Endeavour* some 100 people were gathered: artists, cartographers, astronomers and naturalists. The voyage had royal approval and was financed by the millionaire industrialist Sir Joseph Banks. The holds were crammed with all sorts of scientific equipment and enough provisions to last for a year. The voyage was one of a series of voyages aimed at working out exactly how far the earth was from the sun, by observing an eclipse of Venus from different points on the globe.

Cook's mission was to observe the eclipse – which the famous astronomer, Edmond Halley, predicted would occur on June 3, 1769 – from the Pacific island of Tahiti. But Captain Cook had another aim in mind when he set sail. He wanted to find the continent of *Terra Australis*. In the eighteenth century scientists believed that an enormous continent, or *Terra Incognita*, must exist in the southern hemisphere in order to balance the land masses of the northern hemisphere.

Cook chose a good, serviceable collier, a ship designed to transport coal and made by shipbuilders in his native Whitby, rather than a more elegant, but less reliable, frigate. He was also very careful about his choice of provisions; lemons, oranges, pickled cabbage and onions were served regularly on the voyage to prevent anyone getting scurvy. After seven months at sea it was a very healthy team which arrived at Tahiti, right on time to observe the eclipse. With the main task completed, Captain Cook then set off southwards until he came to the coast of New Zealand. At first he thought it was the coast of *Terra Australis*. He sailed the length and breadth of the two islands, making a very precise map of the land and the straits between. Then he sailed northwards up the entire east coast of Australia, but found the land was not as large as people had expected.

On his return to England, in July 1771, his voyage was hailed as a triumph. He brought back really accurate maps of all the lands he had visited, drawings and descriptions of the native peoples and the flora and fauna. The voyage also convinced Cook that a large continent could not exist south of the Equator unless it was much farther south than he had gone.

To prove his theory he undertook a second voyage and, from July 1772 to July 1775, he sailed around the world. This time Cook took with him the first reliable instruments which could be used to calculate the exact degrees of longitude in relation to the Greenwich meridian, and so help to pin-point the position of his ship at any point on the voyage. This was a much tougher journey than the first. His two ships, *Resolution* and *Adventure* went much farther south and touched the Antarctic circle in two places. On each occasion enormous icebergs stopped them going any farther. In his diary Cook wrote that as they approached the ice he could hear penguins, but never actually saw any. He also saw a few other birds which led him to believe he was near land, but he did not believe that anywhere beyond the ice-floes could be habitable. So Cook, who was concerned about his crew in the icy conditions, returned home. He had at least proved that the idea of a vast southern continent was false.

On his third and last voyage, from 1776 to 1779, he aimed to discover a passage between the Pacific and the Atlantic, north of America. He rounded the Cape of Good Hope, passing Tasmania and New Zealand again before crossing the Pacific towards Tahiti. Then he discovered the Hawaiian islands, which no European had ever seen before. He followed the west coast of America northwards right up to the icy waters of the Bering Strait. But he could not cross through to the Atlantic Ocean and so returned to Hawaii.

At first the natives there treated him like a god. But very soon the goodwill that existed between the British sailors and the natives broke down. On February 14, 1779, Captain Cook was killed in a skirmish with the inhabitants. His crew could only recover a few pieces of his body, the rest having being distributed amongst the local chiefs.

Two stories about Captain Cook's life are particularly revealing. Firstly, he took such good care of his crew that he lost only three men between 1768 and 1779. Secondly, his father learned to read, at the age of 84, in order to follow the newspaper reports of his son's discoveries. In his travels James Cook made two major discoveries, that there was no large southern continent, nor was there a navigable passage in the northern hemisphere between the Pacific and Atlantic oceans.

There was nothing in James Cook's (1728-1779) upbringing to suggest the extra-ordinary life he was to lead. The son of a humble farm labourer in Yorkshire, he first worked in a haberdasher's shop. However, he soon realised that he wanted to become a sailor and learned his seamanship with local fishermen aboard their sturdy colliers and whaling boats. Then he joined the Royal Navy, where his leadership qualities soon brought him promotion.

The American Colonies

Many of the North American Colonists would have left behind impoverished lives in Britain to seek their fortune in the New World, where they believed that land was so fertile that working was little more than a game.

To pay for their passage many passengers would have had to work on the ship for the duration of the voyage, only to be sold by the captain of the ship to a farmer. For the next five years such passengers would work but get no wages, although they would be housed and fed. Only after this period would they have been able to strike out on their own and make a new life

for themselves. Some sold everything they had to pay for their families to travel to America, others had no choice, as they were criminals and prostitutes sentenced to deportation in order to provide the new territories with much-needed cheap labour.

By the 1770s the 13 British colonies in North America had a population of some two and a half million people. They were mostly English, with a few Scots, Irish, Germans and French. In comparison, New France, which became a British colony known as Canada from 1763, remained under-populated. Barely 60,000 colonists lived in the Saint Lawrence valley, with the majority around Montreal or Quebec. Apart from Canada, whose wealth lay mainly in its fur trade, most of the northern colonies were largely industrial. New England was mainly agricultural, large quantities of cereals being grown on family-run farms.

These farmers tried to live a simple life, according to their understanding of God's laws. This meant providing themselves with the bare necessities, such as food, clothes and shelter, but not indulging in luxuries. The merchants of Boston, New York and Philadelphia made their living out of trading with England.

As more and more settlers arrived they gradually spread out towards the west. In true pioneering spirit they cleared and cultivated land and built towns. The work was hard but many pioneers soon made their fortunes. This, however, was at the expense of the indigenous population, the so-called "Red Indians", many of whom died from illnesses or from the effects of alcohol brought to them by the Europeans. The remaining tribes were unable to unite to fight the settlers.

In the southern states, however, the picture was quite different. Here rice, tobacco, indigo (a tropical plant that yields a blue dye) and cotton plantations flourished. Plantation owners lived like lords, riding round their estates on horseback. They spent their money on luxurious houses and beautiful clothes for their wives. They enjoyed fox hunting, balls and grand receptions. However, this rich society made its wealth by using slave labour. Nearly three million negro slaves, imported from Africa, worked in the south without any rights at all. They were owned, body and soul, by the plantation owners. Much the same

situation existed in the West Indian "Sugar Islands". All the leading colonial powers owned islands in the Caribbean: Jamaica was British, Guadaloupe and Martinique were French and Puerto Rico and Cuba were Spanish. They grew hardly anything but sugar cane, so great was the demand for it in Europe.

Central and Southern America was owned largely by Spain or Portugal. Brazil was administered from Lisbon, while the rest of the territories were governed from Madrid. There were many natural sources of wealth: gold and diamond mines, the best kinds of wood, sugar cane, cotton, indigo, rice, tobacco, coffee and cocoa. The population was multi-cultural: apart from European settlers, native South American Indians and African slaves, cross-breeding had created new races such as creoles and mulattos. Although they lived and worked side-by-side, there was a very strict ethnic hierarchy, especially in the Spanish colonies.

All the American colonies were tied to their colonial powers and had to conform to strict rules of commerce and trade: each colony could only trade with their coloniser and could produce only those commodities which that country needed. In time plantation and farm owners, merchants and manufacturers at all levels of society started to resent these restrictions. Their discontent was to lead to the American War of Independence which marked the end of the eighteenth century.

This charcoal study by Watteau shows two black boys from the colonies. Amongst the upper classes it became the fashion to have after-dinner liqueurs served by a black page boy. However, several people could see the degrading side of slavery and spoke out against it.

The Iroquois Indians lived along the shores of Lake Erie and in the Appalachian Mountains, their leading tribes included the Mohawk, the Seneca and the Huron. Disputes between the American Indians and colonists were often violent. But gradually, partly due to the introduction of alcohol and European diseases, the native population of North America started to decline.

The Rise of Science in Europe

Thanks to the progress in optical sciences, astronomy made great strides. Being able to watch the stars, comets and eclipses gave everyone a feeling of being involved in exploring the mysteries of the universe. For instance in 1758 hundreds of amateur astronomers watched Halley's comet.

Throughout Europe in the eighteenth century Royal Academies of Science were set up and great strides were made in all branches of science. In astronomy, Sir Isaac Newton's laws of gravity were universally accepted and the idea of an infinite universe grew, as observatories were able to see farther and farther into the skies with the advent of better telescopes.

In physics the mercury thermometer was invented to universal acclaim, although the scales of temperature measurement differed depending on who the inventor was – The Fahrenheit, Celsius and Réaumur scales were all used. Electricity created the most interest. People knew how to generate it by friction and what substances were the best conductors. In France Antoine Nollet, an experimental physicist, performed an experiment in which a line of three hundred monks would each hold an iron bar, and he would pass an electric current along them. Each man jumped in the air as the current passed through him. The American, Benjamin Franklin, tried out his theory that lightning was attracted by rods, and eventually made lightning conductors for many homes. However, some people saw attempts to divert lightning as interfering with God's work: in France this led to a young lawyer, Maximilien Robespierre, defending a young aristocrat who was

charged with blasphemy for using a rapier as a lightning conductor.

The first adventures and experiments in flight were made, with the Montgolfier brothers managing to fly a balloon, carrying a sheep, a cockerel and a duck, from Versailles, near Paris. It landed ten minutes later in the forest of Vaucresson, proving to all the onlookers that life could exist in the higher atmosphere.

In chemistry the name of Antoine de Lavoisier of France was among the most important. The son of wealthy parents, he spent £10,000 and all the time he could spare from his job as a regional tax controller, in his laboratory. He was among the first to produce theories on the composition of air and to identify oxygen and nitrogen.

Important work was also done in the field of natural science, notably by Georges Louis Leclerc, Comte de Buffon (1707–1788). Curator of the Royal Gardens, he compiled an enormous 44-volume work on all aspects of natural and earth sciences. The first volume of his *General and Particular Natural History* appeared in 1749 and the last in 1804, some 16 years after his death. Buffon was the first of the French writers of the Age of Reason to question the Biblical version of the creation and evolution of the world. He set the age of the earth at more than 70,000 years, against 6,000 by Biblical reckoning, and questioned the doctrine that God created the world in six days. He went even further, showing that all varieties of life – animal, vegetable and mineral – were interdependent and had evolved gradually. He put forward the first theories of man's descent from apes that Charles Darwin developed in the next century. In 1751 the faculty of theology at the Sorbonne told him to retract his ideas as they were contrary to *Genesis* – the opening book of the *Bible*. He agreed, but never gave up his own belief in his theories.

The spirit of scientific enquiry, where it flourished, still met with serious opposition. Only a small

minority of people believed in the new scientific discoveries. Both the Church and the uneducated population were quick to condemn many of the new ideas. In one place there were even reports of country folk chasing after an escaped balloon in the belief that it was some sort of fire-breathing dragon. Unfortunately, many scientists did not help their own cause by putting forward some quite extraordinary and very mistaken theories. Voltaire himself swore he had seen a shellfish being born in the middle of a field.

Confidence in the new discoveries and inventions grew gradually. Soon, it was believed, science would overcome all ills and there would be no more disease, wars or social problems. Above all else, the eighteenth century was the century of optimism.

In 1752 in Philadelphia the American scientist, writer and statesman Benjamin Franklin (1706-1790) flew a kite into a thundercloud to find out if lightning and electricity were the same thing.(Mansell Collection.)

Joseph Cugnot's carriage, built in 1771, was one of the first attempts to build a steam-powered vehicle. However, the machine was not easy to steer and a greater problem was that the boiler needed refilling with water every 15 minutes.

Fighting Intolerance

There were many people in eighteenth century France who did not want the status quo challenged especially in the government and the Church, the two main establishment institutions. However, the philosophers, as the leading reforming writers were called, wanted to be governed by the laws of reason, as they saw them, and not by the dogmatic beliefs of the Church or the prejudices of powerful government ministers. In 1721, Montesquieu had attacked these two institutions in an allegory about Eastern rulers. Gradually the philosophers became more daring in their criticisms, risking imprisonment in the Bastille, exile or excommunication. Their ideas were to influence not just France but many other European countries.

This bust by Houdon has captured the lively spirit of a very unusual man. During his lifetime Voltaire was a celebrity. Countless famous people visited him at his retreat at Ferney. They came from all parts of the world to consult or simply to see the great man. His death in 1778 was felt as a great loss.

The most fiery of all the French critics was undoubtedly Voltaire. Voltaire was the pen-name of François Marie Arouet, who was born in 1694, the son of a lawyer. He received a good religious education from the Jesuits, but from the age of 23 he was regularly imprisoned in the Bastille for expressing his opinions. However, imprisonment, exile and the burning of his works only made him more determined. He loathed the blind obedience of those he saw around him and spent the whole of his life writing scathing condemnations of injustice, despotism, torture and the suppression of free thought.

Unlike the other philosophers, who were content just to put their ideas in writing, Voltaire became actively involved in bringing about reforms. From 1761 to 1765 the Calas Affair shook the nation. Jean Calas was a Protestant from Toulouse who came home one night to find his son hanged. The local parliament followed up the case immediately, accusing Calas of murdering his son because the latter had been on the point of becoming a Roman Catholic. Calas was found guilty and executed. The Protestants asked Voltaire to take up their cause, insisting that the son had committed suicide. Voltaire demanded a pardon for Calas and wrote to many European leaders for support. He eventually won and Calas was pardoned posthumously.

Voltaire also fought the cause of a young nobleman and Roman Catholic, the Chevalier de la Barre. The Parliament of Paris condemned him to death. A copy of Voltaire's *Dictionnaire Philosophique* was burned with him. What was the man's crime? The reason given officially was blasphemy, as he had been seen to spit upon a crucifix, but the philosophers believed it was because he had become too influenced by their writings against the Church. Voltaire again pleaded the cause of a dead man, but this time in vain.

Although most of the philosophers were opposed to the dogmatic teachings and laws of the Church, they were by no means atheists who did not believe in the existence of God. They simply saw him as something other than a bearded overlord or a body on the Cross. For the Deists, as this group was known, God was a supreme, universal being endowed with knowledge of everything. All wars, persecutions and crusades in his name were merely the results of human selfishness and pride.

As well as religious intolerance, the other target of the Enlightenment writers was despotic and authoritarian power. They believed all men should have the right to believe, act and think as they liked and that all men be treated as equals. The philosophers of the age urged all European leaders to adopt a policy of religious tolerance, and to put a stop to all practices, such as slavery and serfdom, which were against the idea of human equality. They even demanded that the privileged classes should be taxed in the same way as other members of society.

However, they were undecided on what actually constituted the ideal form of government. The example of the English constitutional monarchy – with its separate legislative, executive and judicial bodies – greatly appealed to many of them. Others thought that enlightened despots were permissable, especially if they were monarchs who were trying to modernise their countries. It was only Rousseau who extended his ideas to the point of advocating total democracy.

Despite all the opposition the new ideas slowly became accepted and were adopted in many European countries. And the writings of the philosophers inspired the leaders of the French and American revolutions.

On the execution, in 1766, of the 19-year-old Chevalier de La Barre, Voltaire commented: "To condemn to death a man, who deserved at the most three months in prison, was the act of unjust tyrants, or rather fanatics, who, when they have the power to implement their ideas, invariably become tyrants".

The *Encyclopaedia*

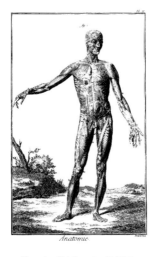

Denis Diderot (1713-1784) was one of the most famous men of the Enlightenment. The Encyclopaedia *was an attempt to produce a résumé of all the knowledge of his time.*

With its seventeen volumes of text, eleven volumes of illustrated plates, dozens of distinguished contributors, 71,818 entries from A to Z, 25 years of work, 4,300 subscribers after the first edition, six reprintings and 24,000 copies sold by 1789, the *Encyclopaedia* was indisputably the best-seller of the eighteenth century.

It all began in 1745 when the bookseller and publisher Le Breton undertook to produce a French edition of a British work, Chambers' *Cyclopaedia*. Two years later, Denis Diderot and the mathematician d'Alembert became co-directors of the

project and planned a much more ambitious work. Diderot's contributors believed him to be the most ardent defender of the Enlightenment. They even bailed him out when he was imprisoned at Vincennes, in 1749, after the publication of his political satire *Lettre sur les Aveugles* – A Letter on the Blind.

Under Diderot and d'Alembert the *Encyclopaedia* changed from a short, general reference book to an enormous work, which contained the most recent discoveries and theories from every field of knowledge. Entries were also commissioned from the leading writers and experts of the day, such as Voltaire, Rousseau, Turgot and Grimm.

The *Encyclopaedia*, while covering every branch of learning, was also a powerful tool in the fight against the forces of traditionalism which opposed progress. The tone was set in the foreword to the first volume, which appeared in 1751. It claimed that knowledge of the world could only be gained by use of the senses, aided by memory and imagination. Religion could not determine truth, it maintained, and added that neither the Church nor the State had the right to decide what men should or should not know.

In the main body of the book, however, the contributors took care not to criticize the establishment directly. For instance, there were no controversial passages in the main entries under headings such as "Church" or "Christianity". But, in other sections, writers could disguise their criticisms in such a way that it was possible, by reading between

the lines, to gather what the writer was really trying to say. For instance, the "Taxes" entry called for a change in the tax laws; equal taxes for all and the removal of special privileges for the nobility.

Verrerie en bois.

Marine, Forge des Ancres.

Most important of all, Rousseau outlined many of the ideas from his book *The Social Contract* in the entry entitled "Economics".

Anyone who wanted to retain the old regime opposed the new ideas. Everyone from the Jesuit Order, the Jansenist movement, the General Assembly of the Clergy, the Paris Parliament and the King's Council right up to Pope Clement XIII himself, were shocked and insulted by entries in the *Encyclopaedia*. But this only caused Diderot to remark, "among all those who set themselves up as censors of the *Encyclopaedia* there is hardly anyone who has the talent to contribute a decent article to it". Even so, from time to time the editors suffered serious set-backs in their work. The worst crisis came in 1759 with the publication of Helvetius' *De l'esprit*, which gave rise to fears of an upsurge in atheism. So great was the outcry that a royal decree of 1746, allowing the work to be published, was cancelled. Furthermore, the book was put on the Index – the Church's list of banned works – and all Roman Catholics were ordered to burn any copies of it that they possessed.

Eventually the outcry died down and the work was able to reappear, thanks largely to the patronage of two very influential people: the King's mistress Madame de Pompadour and Chrétienne-Guillaume de Lamoignou de Malsherbes. The former appealed directly to the King himself on behalf of the encyclopaedists, whilst the latter, in his capacity as national censor of books and the press, was able to calm the more violent opponents of reform.

Several contributors, who did not agree with such strong atheistic ideas, and who were afraid of the Church's opposition, stopped writing for the *Encyclopaedia*. This left Diderot as sole editor, with Jaucourt as his assistant. Diderot was furious when he discovered that several of his contributors had become cautious and had begun to censor or tone down passages in their work because of the scandal. In the end, after devoting 25 years of unpaid time and effort to the project, he became completely disillusioned with it and declared that the *Encyclopaedia* was nothing but a monstrosity, which should be rewritten from A to Z!

The judgement of history, however, has been much kinder to the work and it has taken its rightful place amongst great victories of the freedom of thought over single-minded censorship.

Marine, Batiment appellé Hourte.

D'Alembert (1717-1783), like most of the philosophers of his day, had a broad range of interests. A mathematician and physicist, he also wrote articles on music and literature.

Verrerie en bois.

The Philosophers' Influence in Europe

Madame de Pompadour, the Duchesse de Maine, Madame de Lambert, Madame de Tencin, Madame du Deffand and Madame Geoffrin were among the leading hostesses at the salons. In this way they were able to take part in intellectual discussions without behaving in a manner that society would not expect from their sex. The Comte Guibert wrote about one of them, Julie de Lespinasse, "Her achievement lay in bringing out the intellectual best in others: she enjoyed that more than revealing her own wit".

In the eighteenth century France was the centre of European culture. Many countries conducted their diplomatic negotiations in French; even the Russians and Turks used it to draw up treaties between themselves. Many foreign writers, such as the German Grimm and the Irishman Hamilton, wrote their original works in French. Leading philosophers and thinkers preferred to work in Paris, where nearly 15,000 foreigners lived in the Saint-Germain district alone. The Swiss-born Jean-Jacques Rousseau, Benjamin Franklin from America and David Hume from Scotland all loved Paris life. "Paris is the only place where one can live", wrote the famous Italian adventurer Casanova, "anywhere else one merely exists."

The capital was full of meeting places where thinkers and scientists could exchange their latest discoveries and ideas. Fashionable cafés and coffee houses were used by poets and writers who gathered to discuss the latest successful play, book or opera. The salons were more exclusive: they were meetings in private houses to which one needed an invitation from the lady of the house to be admitted. Each patroness had her own "at home" days, her own special interests and her own circle of distinguished guests. In the rue de Bellechasse, Madame de Lespinasse's evenings were enlivened by the encyclopaedists. The cultural society of Paris would regularly meet there to put forward their ideas or present their latest verses to a privileged audience. The cultured and fashionable ladies who ran the salons made sure the gatherings were lively and entertaining. They were strong personalities, very liberated for their day, who often wrote books and articles themselves.

The French philosophers also travelled throughout Europe, anxious to learn about the current ideas and discoveries of other countries.

They kept in touch with each other by letter. Voltaire probably held the record – nearly 15,000 of his letters are still in existence, although many were lost. Their published works were also widely circulated abroad. Subscriptions to the *Encyclopaedia* came from many countries and Voltaire's *Zaire* ran to more than 20 English editions.

Magazines kept an ever-increasing number of readers informed about political, literary and artistic events. The Dutch enjoyed a free press and flooded Europe with periodicals written in French. Britain produced up-to-date, high quality publications. The first popular daily newspaper, The *Daily Courant*, appeared in 1702 and *The Gentleman's Magazine*, a monthly publication of nearly 50 pages, covered world-wide news. In France, the *Mercure de France* and the *Journals des Savants* were less ambitious journals.

The idea of nationalism scarcely existed for the philosophers who were interested in the international exchange of ideas. As Rousseau said, "Today there are no longer Frenchmen, Germans, Spaniards or even Englishmen... only Europeans". The philosophers forecast a more humane society in which everyone would be free and equal. In Britain it was considered part of a young gentleman's education for him to make the "Grand Tour" of Europe, in order to learn the latest fashions and ideas.

However, contrary to the hopes of the philosophers, many European countries started to become more introspective. The English had long had their own culture, far removed from that of mainland Europe; France was divided into several regions and the majority of people spoke only in local dialects. As each nation took more pride in its own language, inventions, ideas and culture, the French philosophers' hopes for a united Europe were dashed.

The coffee houses which sprang up everywhere offered a better opportunity to speak one's mind than the politer salons. The leading men of letters met in them regularly.

In the Shadow of Reason

However startling and exciting the ideas of the Age of Reason were they only affected a small number of people. The vast majority of the population could not even read or write – all their culture was passed on by word of mouth. The village remained a tight-knit community. Public proclamations, sermons from the pulpit, pedlars' sales chat and gossip from the trade fairs were all that disturbed the isolation of the village community.

Christianity had long since replaced pagan beliefs but superstitions still persisted. Many people believed that moors and marshes concealed cursed places and anyone foolish enough to venture there would be bewitched without realising it, destined to spread misfortune wherever they went thereafter. In Roman Catholic countries superstitions were often associated with pilgrimage sites which had never even been sanctioned by the Church,

MARIE ANNE COURONNEAU,
*Ayant été Subitement et parfaitement guerie le dit jour 13 Juin 1731.
sur le Tombeau de M. de PARIS, monte son Escalier avec une vitesse
surprenante, portant ses deux bequilles en l'air. 12.*

and these attracted huge crowds. Barren women performed many supposed magic fertility rites, such as gulping down an egg and burying another in a holy spot for a year, to induce childbirth. Many pagan beliefs survived because of their association with miracles performed by saints, for example drinking the water of a spring near a holy tomb, or touching a statue.

It was generally believed that the secrets of nature were known only to a few healers or sorcerers who were endowed with supernatural powers. These powers were considered to be either miracles of God or the works of the devil. In the long evenings village storytellers tirelessly told of fairies, monsters and superhuman adventures. This fantastic and marvellous world was grippingly popular as it offered an escape from the villagers' harsh daily life. The Grimm brothers are probably the best-known of the authors who wrote down many of these tales, which are still enjoyed by children today.

People in towns were also intrigued by the supernatural. In Paris, at the Saint Médard cemetery, the word spread that cures had been performed on the tomb of the deacon. Immediately a crowd rushed in, people were seized with fits, went into trances and whipped

themselves without feeling any pain. Only the closing of the cemetery, and the arrest and imprisonment of the convulsionaries, as they were known, put an end to these disturbances.

Educated people were not necessarily free from such superstitions. Many doctors still tried to cast out the devil by bleeding and purging their patients. They used all sorts of potions made from snakes, crayfish eyes or powdered puppy-dog tails! Thousands of fantastic rumours circulated about pregnancy and childbirth. One of these was that the insatiable cravings of pregnant women left an indelible mark on their children; for example, a craving for mussels would produce a Down's Syndrome baby!

Everywhere incredulity and fear greeted scientific progress. The first lightning conductors were seen as devilish devices which were trying to defy God. The first balloons to land in the countryside were taken for dragons and hacked to pieces. Confidence tricksters exploited such naivety by selling expensive elixirs of youth or love potions. A man from Lyons claimed to have invented watertight clogs which enabled the wearer to walk through water without getting his feet wet. This enterprising fake even sold tickets for a demonstration on the river Seine, but when the day came, he had disappeared and the trusting Parisians got nothing for their money!

In 1731 the reports of sudden inexplicable cures at the Saint-Médard cemetery in Paris drew large crowds of hysterical people. To stop the disturbances the police closed the cemetery on September 29, 1732. As a result, a wag wrote on one of the gates "By order of the King. God is forbidden to perform miracles here".

In 1782, a simple-minded Nottingham labourer called Ned Ludd, destroyed two mechanical looms, claiming they were made by the devil. Poorly paid labourers, with genuine financial grievances, used his name for their Luddite movement, which led to mass destruction of machinery some 30 years later. (Luddite Riots, by Hablot Browne. Mansell Collection.)

The Founding of Modern Russia

Eighteenth century Russia was a huge territory, extending from Sweden to China, with more than 30 million inhabitants, a larger population than any European country. Life in Russia had hardly changed since the Middle Ages. More than 90 per cent of the population were peasants and the great majority of these were serfs. Trading consisted only of a few fairs and the transport of goods from the Far East, such as spices, silks and printed cotton. The few towns which did exist were more like large villages; even Moscow was built of wood and had muddy streets. From the reign of Peter the Great (1672–1725) until the end of the reign of Catherine II (1762–1796), the country underwent a comprehensive programme of modernisation. Peter the Great, who seemed like a giant as he stood more than two metres tall, was an energetic man who travelled, in disguise, through Germany, The Netherlands, England and Austria to look for ways of modernising his country.

As soon as Peter returned to his own country he started to bring society up-to-date in every possible way. He began by cutting off the beards of the nobles who had come to welcome him! The Russians wore their beards long in remembrance of Christ, but the shorter length, fashionable in Europe, was now enforced by law.

Peter the Great's burning ambition was to open Russia to European trade across the Baltic sea. At the end of a long, drawn out war with Sweden, he established a north-western seaboard on the Baltic for his country. There he created St Petersburg, which became the capital city. Russia looked towards the west for its future prosperity.

In order to attain his goal Peter had to make a number of reforms. He set up a permanent army and a centralised administration. The state purse was filled by imposing several taxes based on the French system. In order to create an efficient government he invented a new nobility. In exchange for their service in the army, in government or in industry, commoners were ennobled and given tax-free lands. Finally, in order to clothe and arm his troops he set up new factories. By the end of his reign, in 1725, Russia was producing as much cast iron as England and exporting surplus copper and iron. However, his reforms suffered many setbacks under

Flogging was traditionally reserved for serfs, but Peter the Great was even prepared to flog to death his own son and heir, Alexis, for leading opposition to his reforms.

his successors. Peter had no direct heir and the problem of the succession resulted in a series of bloody conflicts. The situation remained unstable for nearly 40 years until Catherine II came to power in 1762.

Although she had no blood ties with Peter, Catherine II, known as Catherine the Great, showed herself to be a worthy successor. Under her rule territorial expansion continued. Autocratic central and local administrations became more efficient, with good, reliable financial and legal systems. The textile industry, iron and steel production and agriculture all thrived.

However, this modernisation was paid for dearly by the vast majority of the Russian people, who suffered exploitation as serfs. The nobles held complete power over entire villages. They could sell their serfs in "flocks", or hire them out to factories. They levied taxes on them in cash and in kind. This forced labour could last from three to six days a week. Families were split up to fit in with labour requirements. The nobility, on the other hand, were given more and more privileges.

Peasants' revolts were frequent but quickly put down. One of them, however, in 1773, succeeded in shaking the government and the aristocracy.

It started in the smaller countries, where the Cossacks and Bakirs were threatened with Russianisation. It spread to the agricultural and factory workers in the Urals. Pugachev, a former army officer, took charge and called for the peasants to fight the Russian army, promising them liberty and land. Peasants everywhere rebelled, castles were burned and members of the nobility were massacred. In the end military reinforcements succeeded, with difficulty, in re-establishing order. But suppression of the peasantry had only been achieved by a level of violence which claimed an estimated 15,000 lives. Catherine the Great died in 1796. Some philosophers have described her as being an enlightened despot. Her reign of 34 years (1762–1796) showed the true nature of Russian progress to be based entirely on an alliance between the throne and the nobility.

Russian agriculture remained very out-of-date and no progress was made at all. Even the best arable land produced only around 400 kilos of grain per hectare.

The new Russian capital, St Petersburg, was strongly influenced by Europe. The Winter Palace, built between 1754 and 1762, had strong baroque tendencies in its architecture.

Prussia: The Rise of Modern Germany

"Prussia is not a country which has an army, but an army which has a country!" This was the view of Mirabeau, a French politician. Although it was an exaggeration, Mirabeau's words summed up accurately the plans of the Hohenzollern dynasty. For Frederick William I (1712–1740), nicknamed the "sergeant king", had only one idea in mind: to furnish Prussia with an army as strong as that of any other great European power. Two months after coming to the throne, he already had two battalions of grenadiers at his disposal . They were paid, armed and trained from the proceeds of the sale of his father's porcelain, carriages and castles. This was only a modest beginning. In order to procure a large number of soldiers, he needed a large population from which to select them. At that time the lands controlled by the Hohenzollerns were scattered from Poland to the Rhine, and had scarcely two million inhabitants.

So Frederick flooded Europe with pamphlets enticing people to emigrate to Prussia. He paid for their journeys, gave them an exemption from many taxes and, temporarily, from military service. Hundreds of thousands of immigrants arrived. His son Frederick II (1740–1786), known as "The Great", although better educated and more cultured than his father – he was proud of his knowledge of philosophy and was a friend of Voltaire – pursued the same obsessive ideas. At the end of his reign Prussia had a population of more than six million. The population of Brandenburg, another state ruled by Frederick, had tripled. More and more men joined the army. All sorts of tricks were used to enlist them. Some were plied with drink and signed up in a drunken stupor, while others were duped into believing that they would be made officers. Some were threatened physically, while deserters were branded with hot irons. The most effective method of recruitment was compulsory national service, which was introduced in 1733.

The soldiers were led by officers trained at the military academy who came from noble families. Increased financial backing was needed to arm and maintain these troops. New taxes were created, particularly indirect ones, which were levied on many consumer goods as they entered Prussian towns. The kingdom became considerably richer thanks to an active mercantilist policy. The exporting of wool was forbidden in order to help nationalised industry. Coal mining and steel production increased. Large areas of land were improved – the marshlands of the river Oder were reclaimed, and the sandy soil of Brandenburg was irrigated for agricultural production. The two Fredericks certainly succeeded

An ardent Francophile – he claimed he only spoke German to his horses – Frederick II was a perfect example of enlightened despotism which aimed at placing the good of the people above everything. "I am the first servant of the state", he said. He hired the architect Knobelsdorff to build his royal residence near Potsdam. It was called "Sans-Souci", the French for "not a care in the world".

in their nationalistic aims. By 1786 the army numbered 186,000 men and the public coffers were much fuller, containing 55 million thalers (about £10 million). The kingdom benefited from the conquest of Silesia and the successive partitions of Poland.

At the end of the century, in the face of this strict and well-ordered discipline, and probably also as a reaction against it, the first stirrings of the Romantic movement reached Germany. Sentimental writings, which rejected cold reason in favour of the yearnings of the heart and senses, became very popular. Membership of secret societies like the Free Masons and the Rosicrucians, increased. Many people turned to the Church and piety and faith were re-kindled.

The poet Goethe was at the heart of this Romantic revival. Like many philosophers of the Age of Reason he was keenly interested in botany, mineralogy and osteology (the study of bones). He put forward the theory that the jawbone linked man with the animal kingdom. Unlike his contemporaries, however, he rejected scientific experimentation. For him laboratories and analytic devices served only to torture nature. He dreamed of a fusion between man – his senses, his emotions, his intuition – and nature, which for him dominated everything. He wrote in German and often took his inspiration from his nation's past history. His works exalted the torments of men's dreams and passions. The most famous of these was the legend of Faust, the man who sold his soul to the devil to gain the woman he loved.

Prussian soldiers were a force to be reckoned with, thanks to the lengthy drill sessions in which they repeated manoeuvres over and over again, sloping and presenting arms for hours at a time. Any soldiers who could not keep up or in step were punished. One punishment involved making the culprit walk between two ranks of men who beat him across the shoulders to the rhythm of a drum.

Vienna in the Time of Mozart

Vienna was the capital of the Holy Roman Empire, the jewel in the Hapsburg crown. Its brilliant baroque style outshone everything around it. The Empire spread from the North Sea to northern Italy and within it Austrians, Turks, Romanians, Italians, Czechs, Slovenes and Flemish mixed language, religion and dress. And, as the city was the seat of government, all the great nobles lived there. The façades of their houses vied with one another in decoration and sculptures.

The Viennese loved the countryside. Within the forest close to the city were paths, clearings and open-air cafés. On the feasts of Saint Anne and Saint Birgitta, Vienna's patron saints, processions made their way there to the accompaniment of flutes and violins. To satisfy this love of the countryside Emperor Joseph II who ruled from 1780 to 1790 opened up his park and the former imperial hunting lands, which he had had converted into walks, to the ordinary people. He often went there himself, dressed in a plain greatcoat, patched at the elbows, and a cap. He even forbade his subjects to salute him or show any sign of recognition. At the entrance to the park he put up a sign saying "Pleasure grounds. Dedicated to all men by one who values them".

Joseph II's legislation was based on the new ideas of the philosophers. No enlightened despot carried reform further than he did. He forbade the death penalty and torture, abolished serfdom in 1781 and gave peasants the right to own their own property. He guaranteed tolerance and equality to Roman Catholics, Lutherans, Calvinists and the Orthodox churches. He considered contemplative monasteries useless and closed some 400 of them, seized their goods and lands and transformed them into large

farms. He was also concerned about the cultural heritage of his subjects, making German the language of government, even in the kingdoms of Bohemia and Hungary.

To the people of Vienna he gave the Burgtheater, a theatre with a permanent site and a resident company of actors who offered regular performances of a wide repertoire. Amusements could be found in every square, every market place. Barrel-organs could be heard throughout the city and on certain days there were even puppet theatres and mechanical shows. Schikaneder, actor-manager of the suburban theatre Auf der Wieden, put on ambitious productions using sumptuous sets and complicated mechanical props. He even put animals on stage and used hosts of extras to perform extravaganzas like cavalry charges with fanfares and real cannon fire! In all this he was only responding to the public's demand for more and more exotic productions.

Vienna was also the centre of the European musical world. The composers Haydn, Gluck and Mozart all lived there, and numerous private orchestras were formed. The Viennese had applauded Wolfgang Amadeus Mozart as a child prodigy, but as an adult they almost ignored him. Mozart was left struggling and impoverished. He gave music lessons but was poorly paid and his operas at the Burgtheater met with only limited success. These included *The Marriage of Figaro* in 1786, *Don Giovanni* in 1787 and *Cosi Fan Tutti*, commissioned by Joseph II, in 1790. On the other hand, *The Magic Flute*, which was the result of a collaboration with Schikaneder and was sung in German instead of the usual Italian, was enthusiastically received at a suburban theatre. However, Mozart died scarcely three months after the premier at the age of only 35.

Meanwhile the Viennese were going into raptures over a new dance called the waltz. Partners twirled round the floor in a close embrace in a way that no one had ever dared to dance before. At this time Vienna was the most talked about cultural centre in Europe.

Joseph II (1741-1790). "His bearing was that of a soldier and his dress that of a junior officer. His recreation was work and his life was perpetual motion", was how one ambassador described him.

Visits to Two Art Galleries

In France, art remained very much under the control of the Royal Academy of Painting and Sculpture. This body had a virtual monopoly on teaching art and arranging exhibitions. The most important of these were held every two years in the great salon of the Louvre, from which came the term "salon", used to describe art exhibitions. Only artists accepted by the academicians were allowed to show their work.

To Lady Mary ***, August 8, 1781. My very dear friend, I am so sorry that I could not visit you this summer but I just had to be in Paris for the Salon. As you know the exhibition is held every two years in the Louvre Palace and I must tell you all about it.

As usual the Salon opened on August 25, the feast of Saint Louis. Entry is free and the approaches to the Louvre were swarming with people from all levels of society. Ten or fifteen years ago there used to be 15,000 visitors, but now there are more than 35,000. The critics are as scathing as ever and I heard that one gentleman who commissioned a work finally refused to buy it because it was so badly reviewed. Some artists are refusing to exhibit in order to avoid this type of criticism.

The main hall was crammed with people, and on every wall dozens and dozens of paintings hung right up to the ceiling. Louis XVI's portrait received great praise, but I heard a few uncharitable remarks about the pictures of the royal family, saying they had been painted to flatter the subjects and were not good likenesses.

There were also many historical paintings. The Count of Angiviller, Director of the king's buildings, commissions several pictures each year from the best of the academy's artists. He likes to choose pictures that glorify the monarchy. One of the most popular portrays Leonardo da Vinci dying in the arms of King François I. What gratitude in the eyes of the painter! What sorrow in the eyes of the French monarch! It is a painting which arouses people's respect for the monarchy, and you know how much they need this at the moment!

Since Greuze, angry with the

academicians, refused to exhibit at the Salon, you can scarcely find anything original or new. The star of this year's salon is undoubtedly Monsieur David. I had great difficulty in getting through the crowd to admire his *Bélisaire*. The subject of the painting is taken from Marmontel's book, which had trouble with the censors for being too outspoken in its criticism of royalty. The style of this picture is very original and I find it delightful: everyone says that this painter has a great future ahead of him...

...I hope it will not be too long before I see you again, Your ever devoted friend, Annette.

To Annette, Marquise de ***,
September 26, 1781

My dear Annette, Thank you for your lovely letter...we too had our share of good paintings at this year's summer exhibition of the Royal Academy in London.

Burlington House was as full as ever, but mostly with the nobility, many of whom would not know a good picture from a bad one! The Academy's President, Sir Joshua Reynolds, was again the main exhibitor, with a truly original painting entitled *Thais*. Naturally, like all the leading English painters, he also showed many portraits of the nobility.

The great Thomas Gainsborough mixed his portraits with an enchanting new landscape, although no one is too sure where the picture was painted. He and the leading patrons of the academy still disagree about the artistic merit of some of the exhibits, and some say he might even resign!

The most striking new artist was Paul Sandby, whose picture called *View of the Encampment at Blackheath* evoked both praise and censure. Of course William Beechey delighted us, as usual. His *Portrait of a Gentleman* is as good as anything he has painted. But all in all we had too many portraits this year!

Love to you and your family, Mary.

TOP: Thomas Gainsborough, *Landscape with House,* Roy Miles Fine Paintings, London.
ABOVE: Jean-Louis David, *Belisarius Begging for Alms,* Musée des Beaux Arts, Lille.

The eighteenth century was rich in great painters from many countries. In France, Antoine Watteau (1684-1721) captured the spirit of the age with numerous pictures of outdoor parties and by the end of the century Jean-Louis David (1748-1825) had established himself as the greatest exponent of Neo-classicism. From Italy, Antonio Canaletto (1697-1768) and Francesco Guardi (1712-1793) produced wonderful scenes of Venice and other European cities.

Perhaps the greatest painter of the century was the Spaniard Francisco Goya (1746-1828) who painted scenes from everyday life. In Britain the most popular artists of the portrait genre were Sir Joshua Reynolds and Thomas Gainsborough. William Hogarth's many satirical pictures showed the harsher side of eighteenth century society.

Spain: Light Versus Shade

The ideas of reform also spread across the Pyrénées to Spain, but there they were only accepted gradually and with great difficulty. The Spanish way of life, centred on religion and controlled by the Inquisition, was in general strongly adhered to throughout the Iberian Peninsula. Freemasons and anti-monarchists discreetly spread new theories and ideas, but they reached only a very small section of society. The few who did become interested, "Los Illustrados" (the enlightened) came mainly from the nobility.

The situation started to change in 1759 when the "philosopher king", Charles III, came to the throne. He was the second Bourbon to rule Spain and, at the age of 43, had already been king of Naples for more than quarter of a century. He was one of the enlightened despots who encouraged education and tried to modernise his kingdom, especially its agricultural systems. In 1766 restrictions on trading in grain were lifted. Common and municipal lands were given to the peasantry in order to increase the amount of arable land under cultivation. This land was irrigated and canals were dug, under the supervision of foreign engineers. The monopoly which controlled sheep farming (about five million sheep) was broken up to help peasant smallholders. The poor were given craftwork in poorhouses.

The censorship powers of the Inquisition were steadily reduced. The Count of Aranda, a reforming minister, wanted to get rid of the spiritually influential Jesuit order, one of the principal obstructions to the spread of much of the philosophy of the Age of Reason. During the nights of April 2 and 3, 1767, the army surrounded the religious houses of the order and arrested all the priests. Trumped-up charges were brought against them, and they were expelled. Most were sent to Paraguay, in South America, and had their lands in Spain seized.

The king and his advisors gave their protection to "Los Illustrados". Peruvian born Pablo Olavide was one of these. He travelled throughout Europe, meeting Voltaire amongst others, and returned with crates of books. He organised poorhouses for the needy of Madrid, opened a theatre and put agricultural reforms into operation. He even started to set up communes, colonised by Roman Catholic immigrants from Protestant parts of Germany and The Netherlands, to cultivate the barren wastes of the Sierra Morena.

By 1775 there were 13,000 of these new settlers, but Olavide's free thinking shocked many people and the Inquisition gathered evidence and witnesses against him. His trial took place in 1778. He was formally declared

Expelled from Spain, the Jesuits took refuge in Latin America where they ran their missions on the lines of their "ideal society". The native Indians found life in the missions preferable to being sold as slaves.

a heretic, stripped of his possessions and forced to renounce his ideas before being sentenced to live in seclusion in a monastery for eight years.

The fact that none of his powerful protectors made any attempt to help Olavide was evidence of the power that the Roman Catholic Church still had in Spain. The reforming ministers did not really want to cross swords with the Church. When Charles IV (1788–1808) came to the throne, he quickly took some harsh measures: books and pamphlets translated from French were banned as heretical leaving Spain deprived of many progressive ideas for more than a century.

Goya (1746-1828), the son of a workman and an illiterate peasant, managed to enter the highest ranks of Spanish society thanks to his great talent as an artist. He visited the court and received many commissions from the highest ranks of society. (The Swing [detail], 1787.)

51

Jean-Jacques Rousseau

Jean-Jacques Rousseau, a Swiss, was the most radical of all the great eighteenth century writers. His work strongly influenced the theories of the French Revolution (see pages 62-63) and the Romantic movement in European art, music and literature. His mother died when he was born in 1712, and he grew up with his father, a clockmaker from Geneva. He developed a great love of reading and studying, and, in order to enter cultural society, he went to France. He was converted to Catholicism and took up several writing posts – secretary, tutor and clerk at the embassy in Venice. There he saw how arrogant the nobility could be by the way they treated him, a commoner.

Everything changed when he moved to Paris permanently and met Voltaire. With Diderot and d'Alembert he worked on the great *Encyclopaedia* project (see pages 36-37). One day he read that the Dijon academy had chosen as the subject for its next essay prize "Has scientific and artistic progress contributed to the corruption or the

improvement of morals?". This inspired Rousseau to write a brilliant essay opposing the supposed progress which, he said, always depraved human nature. His work won first prize, was published and set him on the road to fame.

He was also a musician and his opera *The Village Fortune Teller* was a great popular success. In 1752 the king and Madame de Pompadour attended a performance and thoroughly enjoyed it. At the royal performance of his opera Rousseau played up his humble origins: he dressed in old clothes, a false beard and an untidy old wig – and refused to see the king when summoned! He did not want to be beholden to anyone. By now he had had enough of Paris and its empty pleasures!

So Rousseau set up house in the country with Thérèse, a simple maidservant. He renounced his Roman Catholic faith and went back to country life. He even tried his hand at writing novels, such as *La Nouvelle Héloise*, a love story which enjoyed great success.

In 1762 Rousseau produced his masterpiece, *Du Contrat Social* (The Social Contract) in which he reiterated his belief that there could be no good government without liberty and equality for the individual. Then, going much further than the other political thinkers of his time, he condemned absolute monarchy and tried to show the uselessness of the aristocracy. The work's opening lines are among the most famous in European literature: "Man is born free, but everywhere he is in chains!".

All this was too much for the establishment: parliament, court, Church were all up in arms. Rousseau's books were burned. He was exiled, slandered and shunned by his friends, even Voltaire. Rousseau set out to defend himself. In *The Confessions*, his first autobiography, he told his life story, outlining his religious beliefs and making no attempt to apologise for, or justify, his actions. On July 2, 1778, he died, submitting his life and works to a God in whom he had never doubted. His work, too modern to be really understood in his own time, is still published and studied today. All his writing was based on the theory that mankind, having been given the necessary qualities by his creator, was capable of achieving freedom, equality and brotherly love.

In contrast to the French philosophers, he had little interest in pure reason, more in feelings and emotions, a view that was at the heart of the Romantic movement in the arts. He put humanity at the centre of nature and then outlined the rights to which mankind was entitled. But, oddly, he did not regard woman as man's equal. This was one of the few prejudices of his age that Rousseau did nothing to oppose.

In Emile, his essay on education, Rousseau gives many examples of his ideas about education. For example, he loses his pupil in the forest of Ermonville when the boy says he is not interested in geography. Eventually hunger drives the youngster to use his wits. He finds his way out of the forest by examining the moss on the trees, a means of finding which direction is north.

Upper-Class Family Life

The idea of family life was venerated in the eighteenth century. Family virtues, such as love between husband and wife and caring for children, were much praised. Diderot wrote of "the immeasurable happiness of domestic life", and loved to see parents and children sharing the same amusements and the same pleasures.

As the Age of Reason progressed, the development of family life was one of the most important social changes in Europe. The poorer classes started to copy the customs of the richer.

In the evening a typical lady of the house enjoyed a period of peace and quiet. She relaxed in a fireside chair, wearing a comfortable dressing gown, and sipping a cup of hot chocolate. Her children and their nurse would have been in to say goodnight. As usual she would have played and chatted with them for a while. As was fashionable at this time, she would have brought up her children on the principles of modern education. The old tutor, perhaps an ageing parson, would have been replaced by a new one, younger and more up-to-date in his or her ideas.

Mothers would now breast-feed their babies instead of using the services of a wet-nurse as they would have done previously. As a caring parent, taking her family duties seriously, a mother would have had to reorganise her life-style; receiving visitors only one afternoon a week and trying to keep the household accounts. To show how proud she was to be following modern social trends, she would have had her portrait painted, with her baby at her breast.

At the end of the eighteenth century the lives of the wealthy town dwellers became more and more centred round the family. In their own homes, private and comfortable, the middle classes and lesser aristocracy were discovering the joys of family life. Although marriages were still arranged by the family, who wanted to join together great names, fortunes or estates, the feelings of the intended brides and grooms were being taken more and more into account. Enlightened parents hoped that at the very least, their son or daughter would agree to their choice. Affection, even love, now existed between husband and wife. Small pieces of jewellery like enamel brooches, cameos or miniatures with the portrait of a husband or wife were all the rage. Locks of hair were worn on the wrist or close to the heart. Romantic novels like Samuel Richardson's *Pamela* were very popular.

Parents became more affectionate towards their children. In place of the rather distant authoritarian approach of the past they cuddled their babies. Couples were having fewer children and could take better care of them. Rooms became smaller and cosier and were adapted to the demands of a smaller family. Large formal dinners gave way to small, intimate suppers. More rooms were devoted to privacy, peace and quiet, like the study, the bedroom and the private bathroom. This was because, as well as enjoying family life, the leisured classes were also caught up in the latest fashion for discovering the inner self. Great ladies wrote detailed personal diaries and autobiographies which like the *Confessions* of Rousseau, laid bare the soul of the author. The portrait painter became a psychologist, stripping his subjects of all outward trappings to reach into their inner beings. The portraits of Reynolds, Gainsborough and Quentin de la Tour and the busts of Houdin bear witness to this new artistic approach. People became less inhibited about showing their feelings in public.

With these changes in home life women lost a lot of their freedom. Now they had to be good mothers, good wives and good housekeepers. Although they had total responsibility for running the home and looking after the family, they were completely excluded from political and business life, denied the right to vote and had their property and money managed by their husbands.

True Happiness, an eighteenth century engraving.

The Difficulties of the French Nobility and Gentry

From 1726 to 1743, when Cardinal Fleury was chief minister, France achieved financial stability. Trade increased and the country prospered. Then, aged 33, Louis XV took the government into his own hands. His way of life scandalised many. He had a long string of mistresses and favourites, among whom the Marquise de Pompadour was the most striking and influential. Thanks to her, royal patronage was extended to the arts. She also offered her protection to the philosophers.

However, financial problems returned. Mismanagement of affairs during the War of the Austrian Succession (1740–1748) and the Seven Years' War (1756–1763) left the national coffers empty. Attempts to impose a five per cent tax on all subjects were defeated by the nobility and clergy, who wanted to keep their right to tax exemption. Choiseul, who was now chief minister, made three attempts to impose a universal tax, but each time parliament refused to enact the reforms. Louis, exasperated by this parliamentary opposition, resumed his powers of absolute rule. In 1770 he replaced Choiseul with three ministers who were prepared to support his own policies. He reduced regional parliaments and local assemblies to little more than courts of appeal in legal disputes. Their political power was transferred to the Crown, and at last the king could introduce the five per cent tax on nobility, clergy and commoners alike. But Louis died in 1774 and his reign ended with its greatest single reform never having been appreciated by his subjects.

When Louis XVI, a young man of high moral standards, came to the throne the aristocracy, some 350,000 people, or one per cent of the French population, owned about 30 per cent of the land. In this social order the

aristocracy and clergy were generally envied and courted. Indeed they led a very pleasant life. But it was not an easy life to obtain: one either had to be born to it or be very rich. There were two distinct types of aristocracy: hereditary families of long standing called the *noblesse d'épée*, and the more recently-created nobles called the *noblesse de robe*. The monarchy was always in need of supporters and so bribed public officials by giving them noble titles. Some such offices could be purchased only at a very high price: counsellor, royal secretary, member of parliament or of the treasury. Nearly 4,000 of these positions existed in the eighteenth century. Rich merchants joined the aristocracy by arranging marriages with impoverished aristocrats. They, or their children, then inherited titles and after two or three generations the family's common origins were forgotten.

Whatever their past might have been, all nobles were entitled to the same privileges. They paid no taxes, had hunting rights and occupied all the higher positions in the army, the Church and the judiciary. However, they also had to live like lords, at their own expense. If they took ordinary jobs they could lose their noble rank. However, there were many levels of nobility. There was little in common between the nobles at court – some 4,000 of them living in luxury at Versailles – and the vast majority of the provincial nobility and gentry who were poor, in debt and had great difficulty in maintaining their status. Times were becoming increasingly hard for them and they were becoming impoverished. The growing incomes of the common people were gained at the expense of the aristocracy. Land taxes were no longer sufficient to keep the nobleman in his high lifestyle. But what could he do? Trade, money-lending and industry were forbidden to him! Life became simply a matter of survival. Some became gentlemen farmers in the English fashion, some became involved in business which was not subject to the law depriving them of their noble rank, while others invested their capital in thriving companies.

In the provinces, country gentlemen revived old privileges. They clung on

to their hunting rights and their judicial powers. They enclosed common lands under all sorts of pretexts. Moors, wastelands, swamps and commons fell into their hands and local farmers were taxed for using them. In many places relations between nobles and peasants became dangerously embittered.

Yet the higher nobility managed to retain the best paid administrative posts. In 1781 officer cadetships were only offered to the *noblesse d'épée*. Some 80 per cent of bishops belonged to families who could trace their nobility back more than 200 years, compared with 50 per cent under Louis XIV. They all resisted any policy of financial equality and fought only to keep their own privileged positions as counsellors to the king.

In the second half of the eighteenth century relations between the nobility and the peasantry were often brittle. The old feudal rights were still an important source of income for the lesser members of the aristocracy who defended them strongly. They did not hesitate to revive old customs and exact tolls and taxes for using bridges, mills, wine presses etc.

Middle Class Discontent

Pierre Augustin Caron de Beaumarchais (1732-1799) led a life that was worthy of any cloak and dagger adventure story. In turn a clock-maker, teacher of the harp to Louis XV's daughters, secret agent and the owner of a vast fortune gained through two marriages, he drew upon his experiences to create the characters for his two greatest plays: The Barber of Seville *(1774 and* The Marriage of Figaro *(1784). Arrested at the start of the revolution, he saved himself by getting rid of his fortune and fleeing to Hamburg. He returned to Paris in 1796, and died there three years later.*

In eighteenth century continental Europe, those who were neither members of the clergy nor of the nobility were deemed to be the common people. This was by far the majority of the population, ranging from the professional classes of lawyers, doctors, bankers, merchants and industrialists to the poorest beggars, peddlars, agricultural labourers and street sweepers. In fact the only thing that this enormous cross-section of society had in common was that they had to pay taxes, either in the form of money or goods, to the state, to the Church and to their noble landlords.

At the heart of this group the merchant class was becoming more and more important. The increase in population, the growth of towns and

Figaro:

"Count...because you are a great lord you believe you must also be a very clever man!...Nobility, fortune, high rank, stately homes, you are so proud of all this! But what have you done to earn such things? You have only been put to the bother of being born, nothing else."

Voila ou nous reduit l'Aristocratie

the expansion of industry swelled their ranks. There were many levels within the merchant class, from the small craftsmen to the big businessmen. The small world of artisans' guilds, which included trades as different as coopers, carpenters and wigmakers, provided craftsmen with the opportunity to build up a successful business. But the higher middle class was very clearly dominant. These professional men, cloth-merchants, accountants, doctors and lawyers, felt they belonged to an élite of talented men who devoted their lives to their work.

The main aim of the rich middle classes was to save enough money to stop being middle class, in Britain by buying land and in France by buying into the nobility. In any case, whether they achieved this or not, they lived like gentlemen in every way. If they had sufficient means they stopped working and lived off their investments. They invented their own coats of arms which they inscribed on plaques to place above their mantlepieces or on the doors of their carriages.

The middle classes began to take a great interest in cultural life. Leisure activities, previously reserved for the aristocracy, were now open to anyone who could afford them. Concert halls, theatres and opera houses were soon open to anyone who could pay for a seat. Like the aristocratic families, they had their portraits painted and hung pictures on their walls. Their libraries were every bit as good as those of the nobility. Their tastes slowly began to affect the arts. The plots of operas, plays and romantic novels no longer took their themes from classical mythology but from family life, and they frequently ridiculed the aristocracy.

In art, paintings of a virtuous nature were very popular. Everywhere basic middle class morality, founded on thrift and honesty, was being adopted. Men's fashions became simpler. For example lace ruffles disappeared, along with satins and bright colours. Sombre, functional attire was more the order of the day for a businessman who worked in an office. Even the nobility gave in to the taste for simpler fashions as they swapped their swords for canes with engraved heads. Everything that was simple, natural and moderate became fashionable.

In France, little by little, due to their increasing wealth, greater numbers of the middle class made their voices heard. They wanted to reform social customs and, in fact, the country itself. Philosophers, who were just ordinary people, like Rousseau or Diderot, put their hopes into words. Soon members of the highest middle class felt themselves to be the equal of the nobility. And, more importantly, they earned their wealth through their own endeavours. They were no longer willing to be kept out of the highest posts of the army, the administration or the judiciary. The financial difficulties of the kingdom only served to convince them that it was time for

them to take control. They were the people who knew how to manage money, and were shocked when the court salaries were published. When a meeting of the Estates General was summoned in 1789, they arrived determined to get the reforms they wanted.

Figaro:
"How I wish I had hold of one of these nobles...! I'd show him that all the nonsense that is printed about him is of no importance at all, except insofar as he can censor it. For where there is no freedom to criticise, writing ceases to be a eulogy and becomes mere flattery. It is only a small mind that sets store by this type of praise."

Marcelina:
"Even in the highest ranks of society women are treated with hypocritical respect. Many are deceived by apparent concern for their well-being, but in reality we are all servants. Men pat us on the head when we are good but punish us severely when we displease them."

In The Marriage of Figaro *Beaumarchais severely criticises the society and morals of his time, Immediately banned in the theatre, the play was still widely read. It supported the many grievances of the eighteenth century bourgeoisie in France.*

59

The Birth of the United States of America

On December 16, 1773, the port of Boston, in the colony of Massachusetts, was in a state of great agitation. Larger and ever more excited crowds were cramming onto the quayside to watch a rather unusual scene. Young demonstrators, disguised as Red Indians, so as not to be identified, were boarding British ships and throwing their cargoes of tea overboard! The crowds applauded and encouraged "The Boston Tea Party".

The incident happened because of the tension which had been building up for some time between the American colonies and their British rulers. The Franco-British war in North America had been very expensive and the English parliament was trying to pass on this cost to the American colonists, as they were the main party affected by the conflict. The American colonists saw that their economic interests were being threatened and refused to pay the taxes levied by parliament in England, a parliament in which they were not even represented. A new duty on tea – which they were forced to import from England – only increased their anger. As a result of the demonstration the British government took a hard line. The port of Boston was closed and the colony was ordered to be governed directly from Britain.

This was too much for the Americans! All 13 colonies united

The tea tax, which gave the British government a monopoly on this trade, infuriated the members of the "Sons of Liberty" society. Dressed as Red Indians, they boarded three British ships in Boston harbour and threw the cargo into the sea.

against England and a protest movement was quickly organised. Traders decided to boycott British goods and each colony sent a

In 1781 the rebels surrounded the English army at Yorktown. After a three-week siege the 6,000 redcoats surrendered. Henceforth the Americans were effectively masters of their own country. (The Siege of Yorktown, by Couder, Versailles Museum. In the centre of the picture George Washington can be seen standing between La Fayette and Rochambeau.)

representative to the first American Congress. There they decided to resist British control, using arms if necessary. And so began, in 1775, the first war of colonial independence. George Washington had the difficult task of recruiting and leading the rebel army against the British redcoats. A young lawyer, Thomas Jefferson, drew up the declaration of independence, on the orders of the congress. Adopted on July 4, 1776, it confirmed the split between the British monarchy and the United States of America, who wanted to be free and independent.

The year of 1778 marked a turning point in the struggle as other European countries joined in the conflict. France, Spain and The Netherlands, three maritime powers, united to oppose British supremacy in America. In 1783, the United Kingdom finally had to recognise the existence of the United States. After many negotiations, the 13 former colonies gave themselves, by constitution, a federal authority. The legislature was split into two houses, the Senate, composed of two delegates per state, and the House of Representatives, whose number varied according to the population of each state. It was decided for the purposes of calculating the numbers of representatives, that a black man was worth three-fifths of a white man. This cynical fraction increased the representation of the southern states and showed that the constitution recognised slavery even though it was banned in several northern states. The president, who was elected for four years, acted as the chief executive. In 1789 George Washington was unanimously elected first president of the United States of America.

So, for the first time, a new nation had freely chosen a non-monarchical, constitutional government along the republican lines advocated by the philosophers of the eighteenth century. Many people in Europe thought it was an example that ought to be followed.

George Washington (1732-1799) was the hero of the struggle for independence and the first president of the United States. Before stepping down, he urged his people not to become involved in European power struggles.

The Old Regime in Crisis

Continually torn between the demands of his courtiers and his own good intentions, Louis XVI did not manage to implement a proper programme of political reform. On the eve of the revolution, however, the king was still greatly respected by the vast majority of his subjects.

The impossibility of splitting the burden of national taxation equally between the three estates – clergy, nobility and commoners – proved the ultimate insurmountable crisis for the old regime.

Joseph II, the Holy Roman Emperor, said of his brother-in-law King Louis XVI of France, "He is rather weak but not stupid. He has sound ideas and judgement, but is over-cautious and slow to act". He described Queen Marie-Antoinette simply as "empty-headed". The royal couple, however, proved to be more than just a ditherer and a scatter-brain.

The king wanted to improve the living standards of his people, but the years of his reign were to demand even more of him than this. A sovereign of vision was needed to overcome the difficulties of a kingdom beset with social unrest; Louis was only an ordinary man. Faced with increasing difficulties he hesitated between reform and counter-reform. But the balance-sheet of his reign was not all against him. He surrounded himself with ministers who were genuinely concerned with the plight of the people.

In foreign affairs the American War of Independence provided France with an opportunity to increase its international influence, especially as Benjamin Franklin came to Paris to plead for support for the republican cause. By the peace of Versailles in 1783, through which Britain recognised American independence, France gained prestige from having supported a people struggling for liberty. In many other respects Louis XVI was influenced by new ideas. He accorded Protestants full civil status, and abolished torture, special courts and serfdom in the royal domains. On the other hand he did not support the financial measures of his reforming ministers. Between 1774 and 1789 he employed eight successive finance ministers in an attempt to solve the budgetary crisis. But the king never dared to tax his faithful aristocracy.

In 1774 Louis appointed Turgot as his first finance minister. Turgot believed in equal taxation for all. He began his plans for reform by cancelling the royal edict which obliged peasants to maintain the roads at their own expense, replacing it instead with a tax on the owners of the land. However, the nobles protested so strongly that in 1776 the king dismissed Turgot. His successors were very careful not to repeat the experiment. It became more important to raise aid for the Americans. A royal state lottery was set up and vast sums of money were borrowed. This increased the national debt to the point of bankruptcy and it became an urgent matter to try to reform the economic system. Three attempts to put an end to the tax exemption of the nobility and clergy all failed.

Civil disturbances increased, as in Grenoble on "the day of the tiles" when the local military commander gave in to the mob and allowed the banned parliament to reassemble. Finally the Parliament of Paris persuaded the king to call a meeting of the Estates General in 1789. This assembly, composed of delegates from the three orders of society, had not met since the beginning of the seventeenth century. The idea was welcomed at all levels of society because each expected to benefit from it. The nobles and clergy expected it to safeguard their material and political power and property. The middle class wanted to participate fully in national government, at last, and the peasants were confident that their feudal tithes

and dues would be abolished for ever.

The king and his chief minister, Necker, were only trying to solve the problems of taxation. They had totally miscalculated the mood of the country. In the spring of 1789, hundreds of elected representatives made their way to Versailles from all corners of France, fired with radical ideas and plans for the future. The inevitable confrontation between the third estate, the commoners, and the first and second estates, the nobility and the clergy, was about to begin.

The situation in Europe towards the end of the Age of Reason was quite different from the situation 75 years earlier. The rise of the Eastern countries of Russia and Prussia, now modern, well-armed states, had completely changed the balance of power from a military point of view. The great gains made by Britain in North America and India, despite the loss of the United States, left it the wealthiest and most politically stable country in the world.

The most important difference was the whole way of life and set of social standards by which Europeans now lived. Industrial and technological improvements had revolutionised society. The new ideas, which started with the success of parliamentary democracy in England and which spread through the work of the French philosophers, had made everyone, whatever their social status, aware of their rights and their potential power. Even in the most strongly Roman Catholic areas, like Spain and Italy, everyday life was freer and more permissive than it had ever been. In France, the failure of that country to embrace full democracy led to the crippling and horrific revolution in 1789, and the wars of the next 40 years. The country paid very heavily for not practising what its philosophers had preached.

At Grenoble in France, on June 7, 1788, the populace took the side of its parliament, which had been closed and its members arrested by order of the king. The rioters climbed onto the rooftops and bombarded the soldiers with tiles and slates. By the end of the day the authorities had to give in to them.

Music in the Age of Reason

The mid-to-late-eighteenth century saw a complete revolution in the world of music. It was an age filled with musical innovation and genius. Part of the reason for this richness was that public demand increased as ordinary people became interested in music. The princely courts, the higher nobility and the great chapels and cathedrals were no longer the only places where good music could be heard. Works specially commissioned for state occasions or church festivals were no longer the sole means of assuring a composer a good living. Public concert halls and opera houses ensured a run of several performances and, for the first time, scores were printed by music publishers and earned royalties for their composers.

The general trend in society towards individual freedom gave musicians a great deal more scope for experimentation in musical form. A musician's status gradually evolved from that of a craftsman dedicated to the glorification of his patron, to that of an artist who was recognised in his own right. Even so, the leading composers, Antonio Vivaldi (1678-1741), Domenico Scarlatti (1685-1757), Johann-Sebastian Bach (1685-1750) and Jean-Philippe Rameau (1683-1764), all belonged to the tradition of court musicians. Vivaldi wrote each week for the following Sunday's cathedral service and Scarlatti could only write his harpsichord sonatas, considered to be his greatest works, in the spare time available between duties as director of music at the Vatican, and later at the Spanish royal court in Madrid.

On the other hand, the German composer George Frederick Handel (1685-1759) was able to work independently in Italy and then in England, where he took British nationality. Franz Josef Haydn (1732-1809) was Kapelmeister, or Director of Music, to Prince Paul Anton Esterhazy in Austria and did not travel at all from 1761 until his patron's death in 1790 when he was able to tour Europe. Wolfgang Amadeus Mozart (1756-1791) suffered more than most from the authoritarian dictates of his patron, the Archbishop of Salzburg, for whom he worked from the age of 13 until he was dismissed for impertinence in 1781.

During the first 70 years of the eighteenth century Italian opera was favoured throughout Europe, with the sole exception of Paris. French audiences preferred "Opera Seria", with its lengthy narratives between occasional arias, and dreary plots taken from Greek mythology. However, in Madrid, Vienna, Venice and London, "Opera Buffa" in the Italian style, livelier in music, plot and acting, thrilled the opera-goers. In some cities those who supported the monumental operatic styles of Scarlatti waged a war of words on the comic farce ("buffo") style of opera which began with the Italian composer Giovanni Pergolesi (1710-1736). The audience would usually watch from boxes with curtains,

Chamber music was born in the palaces of minor princes and the rich bourgeoisie. Often the children of the family would join their music teachers in performing serenades, or, at times divertimenti and other works for small groups of musicians.

A well-known lute player from Cremona in Italy, Antonio Stradivarius (1644-1737), made violins for all the principal courts of Europe. Unequalled for perfection of tone, a few hundred of his instruments still exist in museums and collections, or are privately owned by famous violinists. (Still life with Violin, by Jean-Baptiste Oudry, Louvre Museum, Paris.)

which they could draw for privacy during intervals or less entertaining parts of the drama.

The variety of opera being composed during this time reflected the variety within the opera-going public. Yet whenever opera was performed one thing remained the same – it was always the most popular form of public entertainment. The large European cities had grand opera houses – London's Haymarket, the Opéra at Paris, the Burgtheater in Vienna, the San Carlo at Naples and Teatro Regio Ducale (later La Scala) at Milan.

It was first Bach and then Haydn and Mozart, however, who revolutionised musical form. Bach's organ works set the standard for versatility in composition. Haydn transformed the symphony into its modern form, and is often credited with inventing the string quartet. Mozart's genius lay in all branches of music; most of his 27 piano concertos, 41 symphonies, seven major operas, chamber music and greatest masses are all performed as often today as they were in his lifetime. When he died, aged 35, he left behind more than 620 major works.

Architecture in the Age of Reason

Belgrave Square, London. Like many of London's most beautiful squares, this is in the Palladian style which came into fashion towards the end of the eighteenth century.

The start of the eighteenth century heralded the end of the Baroque style of architecture in Europe. The very rich interior decoration of Roman Catholic churches and monasteries, built during the first decade of the century, was particularly striking. Designed to impress the faithful, it suggested an endless meditation on the vision of the joys of paradise. Everywhere there were spirals, scrolls and garlands, stuccoed colonnades, trompe-l'oeil murals and marble and wooden inlays.

Secular architecture was equally extravagant in its design. Versailles was the model for many great European buildings. There were few continental courts that did not want to have their own copy, and even the rulers of the tiniest principalities in Germany imitated the palace, but on a smaller scale. Such castles, palaces and stately homes were typified by their broad sweeping avenues of trees, their carefully set-out parks and lakes and their formal gardens. The Belvedere in Vienna, designed by von Hildenbrandt between 1720 and 1724 for Prince Eugene of Savoy, had no fewer than seven terraces leading up to it. In the main entrance hall huge statues supported vast vaulted ceilings. The best example of this style in Britain is Blenheim Palace near Oxford, built as a gift from the nation to the Duke of Marlborough for his military victories during Queen Anne's reign.

Gradually the popularity of the Baroque style waned. It developed into the Rococo style which claimed to be inspired by nature and wildlife: shells, corals, scalloped leaves and visions of a dream-world were popular motifs. It was most often associated with the revival of classical architecture. Rococo decorations were used to make the interiors look light, elegant and delicate. Such decorative art lent itself well to the growing demand for a new variety of buildings. In addition to religious buildings and princely mansions, more and more houses were built by the rich middle classes who were anxious to display their wealth and social prominence.

A return to Classical forms was adopted from 1750

The place de la Bourse (stock exchange) in Bordeaux was built following plans outlined by Gabriel, and is a good example of eighteenth century French urban architecture.

onwards, particularly in France and England. Thinkers of the Age of Enlightenment played an important part in this move away from Rococo affectation with their demands for logic, clarity and simplicity in life and art. To fit in with the popular adoption of this rule of Reason, architects took their inspiration from the precise, geometric shapes of ancient Greece and Rome. Façades were more sober; straight lines and symmetry were predominant. Neo-classicism, as it was called, was part of the fashionable discarding of unnecessary ornamentation. Classical structures such as porticos, rotundas, Doric and Ionic temples were all the rage and were often dotted rather unsuitably around the gardens of mansions and stately homes.

The greatest influence on British architects at this time was the sixteenth century work on architecture written by Andrea Palladio, *Quattro Libri dell'Architettura*. From him the name "Palladian" was adopted to identify the new style. The Baroque and Rococo styles, which had inspired much German architecture, seemed extravagant and even debauched to eighteenth century Britons. A return to these Classical principles of architecture suited the British taste for solidity, respectability and lack of affectation. In the later years of the century many English gentlemen added lakes and bridges to their parks, and rebuilt their houses in the Palladian manner. A Neo-Palladian house with its dressed stonework and Classical columns also served to mark the owner's social standing far more obviously than the brick-built gentleman's house of the seventeenth century. On the continent the most influential work in architecture, sculpture

and painting was a treatise on the *Imitation of the Antique*, which appeared in 1755. It was written by Johann Joachim Winckelmann (1717-1768), a German who lived and worked in Rome, and it was about the form and importance of Greek and Roman architecture.

Architects did not just copy classical buildings. Rather, they adapted the style to suit the modern buildings of their day. This was noticeable especially in

public buildings. Town halls, museums, public libraries and great banks and finance houses were all built to be functional as well as to have an architecturally pleasing design. However, buildings did manage to retain their individual character even when built to the new practical designs. They reflected the general trend towards controlled individualism which typified every aspect of the Age of Reason.

Built between 1763 and 1769, the New Palace at Potsdam was almost a Prussian Versailles. Indeed the façade, the rooms with ceilings encrusted with shells and the hall of mirrors were as grand as those at Versailles.

Eighteenth-Century Buildings

Most European rulers from the Age of Reason left behind great buildings or cities to mark their reign. The London of George III is noted for its Baroque and Palladian buildings. Somerset House, near Waterloo Bridge, is one of the finest of these. Many squares contain whole terraces of houses dating from the late eighteenth century. Together with the developments in exterior building was a revolution in interior design which produced many beautiful carved ceilings, doorways and fire surrounds. The most famous experts in this field were the Adam brothers, whose work can still be seen in hundreds of buildings in England.

In Madrid, Charles III completed the Royal Palace and the Puerta de Alcala gate. In Berlin several buildings from Frederick II's time stand out: the great Opera House, the Royal Library and the many avenues of late eighteenth century houses. However, it was at Potsdam

At Charmettes, near Chambéry, Jean-Jacques Rousseau passed the most peaceful days of his childhood. Under the protection of Madame de Warens, he spent his time studying music and reading. Today his former home is a museum.

Just near the Swiss frontier stands the château of Ferney. It contains several souvenirs and mementos of Voltaire who lived there from 1758 to 1778.

that Frederick left his greatest monument, the New Palace, which he modelled on Versailles.

In Russia the best tributes to eighteenth century architecture are to be found in St Petersburg: the Winter Palace, built between 1754 and 1762, shows strong European influences in its Baroque style and the Hermitage Palace, designed for Catherine II. The latter houses one of the world's greatest collections of eighteenth century art.

In France the Petit Trianon palace was built in the grounds of Versailles, where Louis XVI also built a model farm for Marie Antoinette. In Paris the Place de la Concorde and the Elysée Palace, now the Presidential residence, were built during this century. However, throughout England and the continent the biggest change in building terms was the way towns and cities were laid out. Most of our modern street plans have changed very little in the 200 years since they were first drawn up.

Chronology

1715, September 1: Death of Louis XIV

1719 Daniel Defoe writes *Robinson Crusoe*

1720 South Sea Bubble in England and Law's bankruptcy in France

1721 J. S. Bach composes *The Brandenburg Concertos*

1723 Death of the Regent in France. Louis XV gains his majority

1726 Jonathan Swift publishes *Gulliver's Travels*

1733 Start of the War of the Polish Succession

1740 Frederick II becomes King of Prussia

1741–1748 War of the Austrian Succession

1748 Montesquieu publishes *The Spirit of Laws*

1751 Publication of the first volume of the *Encyclopaedia*

1756 Start of the Seven Years' War

1760 French surrender in Canada

1762 Rise of Catherine II in Russia. Rousseau publishes *The Social Contract*

1763 End of The Seven Years' War

1765 Joseph II becomes Emperor of Austria

1768 James Cook's first voyage

1774 Death of Louis XV. Coronation of Louis XVI

1776 American declaration of independence

1778 Death of Voltaire and Rousseau

1779 Death of James Cook on his third voyage

1780 Beaumarchais publishes *The Marriage of Figaro*

Louis XV's writing desk at Versailles.

1782 Anglo-American peace agreement

1787 Mozart composes *Don Giovanni*

1789, May 5: Meeting of The Estates General

Glossary

Absolute Monarchy A system of government in which the monarch has unlimited power.

Bourgeois or **Bourgeoisie** A member of the middle class or the middle class itself.

Constitutional Monarchy A system of government in which the monarch's power is controlled by a parliament or national assembly.

Electors People with the right to vote in parliamentary elections. In Germany "Elector" was also the title given to a prince who elected the Holy Roman Emperor.

Enlightened Despotism Government by an absolute ruler who, nevertheless, brought in many political and social reforms.

"The Enlightenment" The name given to the free-thinking and reforming movement which started in France and spread throughout Europe during the Age of Reason.

Estates General Also called the States General. A French governmental body composed of representatives of the nobility, the clergy and "Third Estate" or the common people. It could only be summoned by the king and did not meet in the eighteenth century until 1789.

Laissez-faire A policy in which a government does not interfere, especially in matters of trade regulations.

Mother Country The term applied by the colonists to a country owning an overseas colony.

Netherlands In the eighteenth century this included most of modern Holland and Belgium.

Parliament In the eighteenth century this meant different things in different countries. In Britain there was only one, nationally-elected parliament which met in Westminster and governed the whole of the United Kingdom and the colonies. In France, however, there were 12 regional parliaments whose members inherited their offices and also proclaimed royal decrees.

Philosopher In the Age of Reason this term meant specifically one of those people who put forward ideas of social, political and financial reform. In its wider, modern sense it means anyone who studies the source, truth, meaning and communication of ideas about life, and the universe.

Revocation Cancelling. For instance, the Edict of Nantes in 1598 brought in new laws of religious freedom in France. These were cancelled by the Revocation of the Edict of Nantes in 1685.

Serf A person who is "bound to the soil". A serf must work in a particular place and can be bought and sold with the land.

Salon Either a meeting of distinguished writers, scientists, painters etc. at a private house to discuss latest advances and ideas in their specialist fields or an art exhibition open to the public.

The Sun King A popular nickname for King Louis XIV of France, derived from the splendour of Versailles.

Index